North Island Trout Fishing Guide

John Kent

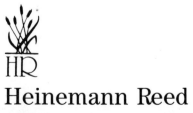

Heinemann Reed

Acknowledgements

I would like to thank my mother Lucy for encouraging my angling interests and accompanying me on a number of field trips, my wife Deirdre for her tolerance during my absence and Robert Bragg of Christchurch who really inspired me to fish as a teenager. My regular fishing companions Peter Bygate and Russell Cockburn of Wellington, Dick Barry, Ron Heslop, John Palmer and the late Wim Van Leuwin of Tauranga, John Brown of Rotorua and Graham Mourie and Shona Fokerd of Opunake all contributed in their own way. I am very grateful for their friendship.

Many people supplied valuable information for this book. They include Dan Hartley and David McLellan of Auckland, Russell Gaston of Mahoenui, David Dannefaerd of New Plymouth, Terry Kelso of Rotorua, and Robert Fenton and Allan Boyce of Hastings. Special thanks to Acclimatisation Society Officers Ian Buchanan of Masterton, Steve Smith of Wellington, Peter Taylor of Feilding and Richard Barker of Wanganui, to officers of the Department of Conservation, especially Dave Stack of Rotorua, for their informed contributions. Finally, my thanks to the farmers of the North Island for their unerring hospitality.

Published by Heinemann Reed
a division of Octopus Publishing Group (NZ) Ltd
39 Rawene Road, Birkenhead, Auckland. Associated companies, branches and representatives throughout the world.

ISBN 0 7900 0049 0

© 1988 Dr John Kent

First published 1989

Designed by Chris O'Brien
Typeset by Typeset Graphics Ltd, Auckland
Printed by Kim Hup Lee Printing Co Pte Ltd, Singapore

Table of Contents

Foreword

Imagine a tall, well-built New Zealander suspended beneath a heavy overhanging branch by two long legs crossed at the ankles. His left hand also holds on to the branch a little further out, while his right arm horizóntally casts a treasured nymph slightly upstream of an unsuspecting rainbow trout. His two dark eyes gaze unflinchingly at his tail-quivering quarry.

This is how you might first see John Kent, the author of this book. Of course, to do this you would first have had to drive or tramp for several hours into New Zealand's remote back country.

Alternatively, you may imagine a tall figure running backwards in lakeside sand, bending low to avoid detection by a cruising rainbow trout. If you bide your time you will see a superb cast unroll from the rod to fall silently into the water. Wait a while and you will see the strike of the rod, hear the triumphant 'Yahoo' and be able to watch the patient but intensely concentrated playing of the fish until it is deftly beached, without the use of a landing net.

Now is your chance to go over and talk to the fisherman, for this one is keen to share all he knows, and that's heaps! Just wander over, say hello, and ask John Kent about fishing. He has been teaching me for over twenty years now.

Read this book and share in his vast experience and knowledge. Whether you are a newly interested learner or an addict of the tantalising sport of fly fishing, John's book has something to offer you.

Pick it up and start reading. See if you can get that big 'brownie' out of the deep-slow-flowing hole in the bend, or maybe you'll pick that dashing rainbow from the tail of the run while sipping your after-dinner coffee. Good luck, I wish I could join you!

Peter Bygate
A Friend
(Deputy Director, Department of Conservation)

Introduction

It has been a privilege to write this book. Many New Zealand anglers with great skill and knowledge have readily imparted their secrets, and I am greatly indebted to them all.

I was brought up on the banks of the River Avon in Christchurch and began fishing for trout with bread, worms and luncheon sausage at the age of ten. At secondary school, along with four other boys, I was caned by the headmaster for 'bunking' a music lesson in order to catch trout from the stream in the school grounds. Being an English scholar, the headmaster at least had the decency to ask if I had read *The Compleat Angler* by Isaac Walton before he administered his punishment.

As a shy thirteen-year-old, I joined the Canterbury Anglers' Club and well remember watching a rotund George Ferris demonstrating the art of casting a fly while lying flat on his back. His skills were beyond my comprehension. At fourteen, I had the great fortune to be introduced to Robert Bragg, a quiet, unassuming Scotsman who earned his living as a fly tier and rod maker. Robert's patience and fund of anecdotes were an inspiration for a gauche teenager. No doubt many of his stories were stretched by his 'anglers' licence', but listening to his yarns while watching him expertly tie up a gross of flies was an experience I will never forget.

My first attempts at fly fishing upset my mother. To supplement my earnings from tomato and raspberry picking, I had pestered her for money to buy my first fly rod. I could not convince her that I needed improved gear. 'You catch plenty of trout in the Avon with the rod you have,' she said. My rod, freshly cut each year from 'bamboo island', had hand-twisted rings of copper wire bound at intervals with black sticky insulation tape. The design came from Tisdalls' sports store. 'Want to buy a rod?' the salesman would ask.

'No thanks, I'm just looking,' would be my embarrassed reply. The old wooden Nottingham reel

1

had been given to me by a neighbour. It had a nasty habit of jamming each time I left it out in the rain, and that was quite often. At the end of each season, my rod would end up in my father's garden firmly staked to a tomato plant. At a family picnic on the shores of Lake Lyndon, I attempted fly fishing. Casting in the approved manner of a fly fisher was out of the question with this rigid bamboo pole and light cuttyhunk line. I propelled the fly like an arrow from bow to land eight metres from the rod tip on a good cast. An angler with sophisticated gear arrived. 'Had any luck, lad?' he inquired, as if he didn't know! He began casting some distance away down the beach. But to my utter astonishment, after ten minutes of 'bow and arrow' fishing, I hooked a takeable rainbow on my Bloody Butcher fly and dragged the fish flapping up the beach. My angling companion had no such luck. 'There you are,' said my mother, in a voice loud enough for him to hear, 'You don't need a new rod after all. That one's perfectly all right.'

When I was fifteen my tramping companion, Skip, introduced me to the baitcaster, a much cheaper method of angling than fly fishing, and a wonderful transition between worms and artificial flies. At least I caught fish! We happily tramped the back country of Canterbury and Otago and became very skilful at using such gear. On more than one occasion, we landed fish weighing over 4.5 kg from isolated high country streams seldom visited by anglers. We used Devon minnows and other more intricate patterns festooned with triple hooks and made by McCarthy's Tackle Shop in Dunedin. Unfortunately, 'birds' nests' were common, as the revolving minnows twisted the nylon line into all manner of knots. At eighteen I purchased my first fly rod and as I gained confidence, the baitcaster was gradually phased out.

My special love is to combine tramping with fly fishing and to visit new water with a good friend. I have been most fortunate in having been able to fish from Fiordland to the Motu. It is difficult to convey to non-angling friends, the companionship, excitement, joy, tranquillity and challenge that back country fishing offers, especially when one arrives home empty handed. The satisfaction of stalking a good fish in gin-clear water, deceiving it with a home-tied artificial, landing it and then gently releasing it is impossible to convey.

There are hundreds of streams, rivers and lakes in the North Island that hold trout. At least 30 streams draining off Mt Taranaki alone contain fish. I make no apology for omitting many of these as I have tried to select those that are worth visiting. To describe each run, pool and bend would likewise be impossible, and intricate details about access would fill an encyclopaedia. Hopefully, however, there will be sufficient information to allow you to explore new territory and fish with a degree of confidence. There is no substitution for knowledge gained from visiting 'virgin' water. Do not hesitate to ask other anglers for advice; most Kiwi anglers will be only too willing to help. I suggest you purchase detailed maps from Automobile Associations and the Department of Survey and Land Information.

I have visited almost all the water described, fished much of it, but not all with success. Good luck and tight lines.

A 3.5 kg rainbow from the Ngaruroro River.

Survival, Equipment and Weather

New Zealand is a narrow, mountainous, windy country with unpredictable weather patterns. Weather forecasting is not easy. It is frustrating to the fly fisher to carefully plan a day's fishing, then arrive to find a howling downstream wind preventing any chance of casting. I have described the general direction each stream follows and strongly recommend studying the weather map and obtaining a forecast before leaving for your day's fishing.

In the mountains, special care must be taken with planning routes, carrying survival equipment and informing others of your intentions. Do not attempt river crossings when the river is high. Camp out for the night, miss a day at work but come home alive. Even in high summer, mountain storms are not uncommon. I have spent four days in February camped under a tent fly sheltering from teeming rain and marking the rising river level with sticks. However, we were still able to light a roaring driftwood fire each day as we carried waterproof matches, fire lighters and a piece of car tyre.

Clothing and equipment will obviously vary according to conditions. Stalking smelting fish along a Taupo beach in summer is very pleasant in sandshoes and shorts. Fishing the same area in June may only be acceptable in chest waders, survival-type clothing, balaclava and parka. Books are available on mountain safety and these contain valuable information. The lists given in this chapter are the personal lists I have used for many years and are directed specifically towards the angler.

1. Equipment for a camp out and tramp into the Ureweras, Kaimanawas, Kawekas, Ruahines or the Motu River.

General gear

Small lightweight tent and fly (in summer, a fly alone can be sufficient)

Sleeping bag (preferably down)

Frame pack

Sleeping pad (I use a short 'Porta Pad')
Billies, 2
Knife (fishing or hunting)
Matches (waterproof)
Torch (lightweight)
Pot-mit
Compass (optional)
Towel, toothbrush
Fishing licence

Clothing
Boots (lightweight but must have commando-type sole)
Underwear (one change)
Longs (lightweight but warm)
Jersey (woollen)
Hat (with a brim)
Parka
Nylon over-trousers (excellent for wading with shorts as they protect from wind chill and sandflies and dry rapidly)

Cooker and fuel (fires can be lit in certain areas)
Fry-pan
Fork, spoon, mug, plate
Piece of rubber or Lucifer fire lighters.
First-aid kit
Camera and film
Soap (small piece)
Axe (lightweight)

Sandshoes
Socks (four pairs)
Shorts
Polypropylene T-shirt
Flanellette shirt or warm fishing jacket (with big pockets)
Watch (can be used as a compass)

Fishing gear
Fly rod or spinning rod (a collapsible rod is useful)
Traces
Large plastic bag (for carrying fish)
Spring balance (for optimists!)

Reels and lines
Flies and/or spinners
Polaroid glasses
Eel line (simple line and hook, great for survival)

Food
There is great scope for variety but I choose varying quantities out of the following list. Generally, trout, eel, and occasionally venison (if a rifle is taken) make welcome additions.

Bread (Vogel's or whole-grain style)
Honey
Dried milk
Salt
Porridge (I prefer whole-grain oat varieties)
'Scroggin' (mixture of dried fruit, nuts, ginger, chocolate, etc)
Cheese
Salami

Butter or margarine (also useful for cooking)
Brown sugar
Tea and coffee
Bacon
Muesli
Brown rice
Packet soups
Dried vegetables
Freeze dried meals are optional but useful as a reserve.

2. Equipment for a day's fishing

Clothing can be selected according to the season and area being visited. I tend to wear neutral colours when fishing, to blend in with the background. Green, brown and blue are satisfactory but red and yellow seem to scare fish. When fishing in boots and shorts, I use nylon over-trousers in cold or windy conditions; these also keep the stones out of my boots. On a warm day, I use anklets for this purpose. A shirt or fishing jacket with large secure pockets, preferably zipped, is most useful.

I have a small day pack for carrying a thermos, fishing sundries, knife, camera, plastic bags, spare clothing and of course a good lunch.

Although I own a pair of thigh waders, I seldom use them. If the stream or lake requires waders, I use the chest variety. The new style waders made in the same material as wetsuits are much warmer and more flexible than the old rubbers.

3. Fly fishing gear

Personal preferences govern the choice of rods, reels and flies. I clearly remember meeting an elderly angler on the Tauranga-Taupo River successfully using a double-handed rod the size of a power pole. He showed little interest in my high-tech, lightweight carbon fibre rod. I have owned bamboo, greenheart, split-cane, fibreglass and carbon fibre rods. All have their advocates and uses. However, the powerful lightweight carbon fibre rods are a pleasure to use and are much more versatile. The same rod could be used successfully for fishing a Taupo river-mouth, the Tongariro or a small fly stream. At present I use two rods, both carbon fibre but differing in length and power.

For small streams and back country rivers 2.6 m lightweight rod with a light fly reel holding a double tapered No 6 floating line and 60 m of backing. The reel has an interchangeable drum holding a medium sinking line.

For the Tongariro River and for competing with other anglers at stream mouths 3 m rod and reel holding a weight forward No 9 floating line and 100 m of backing. I have two other lines for this rod, a slow-sinking line and a high-density or fast-sinking line.

Traces or tippets I find Racine Torture and Dai-riki nylon very good although there are many satisfactory brands available.

For dry fly and nymph fishing in clear streams, I use 2 to 3 kg weight.

For nymph fishing on the Tongariro — 3 kg. For lure fishing on the same river — 4 kg.

For night fishing at stream mouths — up to 6 kg.

Flies When I first began fly tying at fifteen, I tied every pattern in C.H. Kendrick's *Modern Fly Dressings*

(1949) and most of those listed in Eric Tavener's *Fly Tying For Trout*. Now I fish with confidence using a few well-tried and trusted varieties, many being modifications of original patterns. However, other patterns can be equally effective. Trout can be most discerning, or rash in the extreme. When schools of Taupo trout madly chase smelt into the shallows, a piece of string tied to a hook will be as deadly as the most sophisticated smelt fly, provided it is handled correctly. There are many flies that have no parallel in nature, yet they take fish regularly.

The presentation and size of the fly, the way it is fished and whether the fish are feeding are factors that perhaps have greater significance than exact attempts to match the hatch. However, entomology as it applies to trout fishing, broadens one's appreciation of the finer arts of angling and Norman Marsh's excellent book *Trout Stream Insects of New Zealand* should have pride of place in every serious angler's library. How many times have you experimented with a new, untried pattern of fly, fished it without conviction or success, then with a sense of relief changed back to an old faithful and immediately had success? Confidence in your fly is important.

Many varieties of insect are enjoyed as part of a New Zealand trout's diet, as is clearly revealed when a freshly caught fish is autopsied. I have found caddis, nymphs of different kinds, cicadas, manuka beetles and mayflies all in the same stomach, yet this fish accepted my artificial fly despite the fact that it bore little resemblence to any of the ingested smorgasbord. When the fishing is hard, however, there is no substitute for careful observation and an innovative approach.

My old tutor, R. K. Bragg, lived on the banks of the Wairarapa Stream in Christchurch. Upstream from his house was a small grassy reserve where families came to feed bread to the ducks. White crusts missed by the ducks floated downstream and were gratefully accepted by fat brown trout at the bottom of Robert's garden. All his attempts to match the insect life of the stream were to no avail. The trout continually ignored his efforts. In desperation, he tied an artificial fly out of kapok made to resemble a wayward crust. Success was immediate, but being a true sportsman, Robert did not have the heart to keep the fish that gratefully accepted his 'kapok killer'.

Some anglers prefer dry flies with wings; others are quite happy with the hackle variety. The latter group I suspect are like me and have some difficulty in tying a neat looking size 14 with wings. My fumbling efforts may well aim towards creating a dry fly but often get reclassified as a nymph, with wings resembling an unopened parachute. Every angler has their tried and tested fly patterns. Here is a list of the ones I have found useful.

Lures

Night fishing

'Bethlehem Cat' tied with two bunches of black cat's fur along the top of the hook and a short tail of similar material. Black squirrel also makes a good tail that does not wrap around the shank of the hook. The body is made of black or red mohair or wool, the topping, two pukeko feathers (optional). Recently, luminous material has been in favour for fly bodies. I have yet to be persuaded to adopt this innovation, but some anglers are certainly in favour of it. I have grown to trust this fly providing it swims well, and rather than change to another pattern when the fishing is hard, I prefer to change the size of the fly. I use sizes 2-8.

Day fishing

Rabbit Flies Sizes 4-10. The body is orange, green, yellow or silver depending on conditions. Fur colour can vary from silver to black.

Red Setter Sizes 4-8. Good all-purpose fly for high country rivers, stream mouths for run fish and for night fishing.

Parson's Glory Sizes 4-8. Can also be tied in similar fashion to a Red Setter (using Honey Grizzle hackle). This prevents feather wrap-round.

These three patterns are good all-purpose lures. I have used them for smelt fishing, river-mouth fishing and high-country lure fishing.

Smelt fishing

Taupo Tiger (modified) Badger hackles tied as a tail fly on a long shank hook. Sizes 6-10. Again, the long shank hook prevents feather wrap-round. The body can be white or grey wool or chenille.

Kent's Smelt Tied in similar fashion to a Doll Fly on a long shank hook. Sizes 6-10. The body is of white floss or wool with a topping of grey wool. Darker shades are used on dull days.

Dry flies

Coch-y-bondhu and *Royal Wulff* Sizes 10-14. These two flies represent beetles prolific on back country streams. The white wings of the Royal Wulff are easily spotted in rough water.

Dad's Favourite, Twilight Beauty and *Kakahi Queen* represent species of mayfly. Sizes 14-16.

Sedge Pattern with sloping wings (these are not difficult to tie and I use deer hair or cat's fur). They represent adult caddis. I use a size 12 long shank hook, although smaller sizes are often very useful.

Nymphs

Hare and Copper, Pheasant Tail and *Half Back* in sizes 12-14. The Hare and Copper tied on a long shank hook with black opossum fur can resemble a creeper or stone fly.

Nymphs are weighted according to the water being

fished. For run fish on the Tongariro, I use liberal amounts of lead and copper wire. Other imitations I find useful include *Midge Pupa, Willow Grub* and *Cicada,* although a large *Coch-y-bondhu* makes an adequate imitation Cicada.

4. Spin fishing gear

Rods
There are various lengths and weights of rod available in most sports shops. A fibreglass rod 2–2.5 m long is recommended. It is an advantage to be able to collapse the rod down so it can fit into a pack. Some telescopic varieties fold to less than 0.5 m.

Reels
The old baitcasting reels controlled by your thumb have been replaced by the fixed-spool reel. These can be either open or closed face. The closed-face reel is ideal for beginners but the casting distance is less than with the open-faced variety. The open-faced reel has a far greater line capacity and snarl-ups are easier to deal with. To achieve maximum casting and retrieving capability, the drum should be filled to capacity with line.

Line
Monofilament line weights can vary, depending on conditions, from 1.5 to 4.5 kg.

Spinners
There are many varieties on the market but a selection of the Toby, Cobra, Flatfish, Penny, Tasmanian Devil, Billy Hill and Zed in different colours and weights is desirable. The smaller Veltic and Mepps spinners are useful in low-water summer conditions. The Tokoroa Chicken has a place in heavy water. Some anglers still use a bubble for fly fishing with spinning gear.

It is important to vary the speed of the retrieve as some fish will follow right into shore and actually pick up the spinner at the angler's feet when all motion has ceased.

5. Boat fishing gear

Full safety equipment is essential when boat fishing. The larger lakes can become very rough and treacherous even for sizeable craft. In half and hour Lake Taupo can change from a mill-pond to a raging sea. I have been embarrassed by these conditions on more than one occasion even in a 5.5 m cabin boat. The same safety equipment for offshore salt-water fishing should be taken on Taupo. This should include an auxiliary outboard, oars or paddles, flares, life-jackets, tool-kit, anchor and warp and a bailer.

Fishing equipment can include boat rods or fly rods, reels and lines, flies and spinners, landing net, fish box and knife.

If an auxiliary outboard is not used for trolling, boat speed can be reduced by towing a bucket or sack.

When using a lead line, remember every 10 m (one colour) will sink 1–2 m. If fishing in 3–5 m of water, use only 20–30 m of lead line. At the end of the lead line, attach 6–7 m of 6.5 kg nylon and then a trace 3 m long and 4–5 kg weight. This will enable fish to fight better and if the line should snag, the lead line will not be lost.

If using monofilament line, a colour or two of lead line can be used to help it sink. (See specific lakes for restrictions and comments.)

Generally, the most productive trolling can be obtained by following the blue line or drop off.

Remember, do not troll within 300 m of a river or stream mouth, and have respect for other boaties by keeping well clear.

Conservation and Etiquette

While collecting information for this book. I have visited well over 200 rivers and streams, and 35 lakes. I have been saddened by anglers' reporting stream deterioration and reduction in the fish population in many parts of the North Island. While I am sympathetic towards land development and drainage for farming, there can be no excuse for clear felling and stock grazing right to the stream margin. Obviously, the cost of fencing off streams from marauding stock is considerable, but I can see no other way of restoring water quality in many places. The leaching of phosphate and nitrate fertilisers is well recognised and proved. Slow-release fertilisers, along with stream buffer zones, would go a long way towards solving this problem. Some farmers even use streams and rivers as rubbish dumps, and I have no great desire to snare a trout out of the back seat of a rusting old car.

The unstable nature of the East Coast, Gisborne and Hawke's Bay high country is well known and contributes to the serious run-off and flooding that so disturbs a trout's environment in those regions. It is imperative that the remaining native bush cover is protected, as often water flow in streams rising from cleared areas is reduced in summer to a point where fish cannot survive.

There are, however, farmers, local authorities, acclimatisation societies and conservation organisations who have cooperated to improve water standards. Lake Tutira is a fine example.

Discarded cans and bottles hardly contribute to the environment unless one is an avid collector of beer cans. I am constantly delighted that although many Taupo rivers are heavily fished, there is very little rubbish to be seen along the banks. Some boat owners using the lake need reminding, however.

Apart from the Lake Taupo fishery, there are very few streams, rivers and lakes that can cope with being heavily fished. Back country rivers and small streams are especially vulnerable. In some waters, limit bags should be reduced to two fish.

As a rule, visiting anglers from overseas are very aware of practising catch and release methods. Many Kiwi anglers need further encouragement. Les Hill and Graeme Marshall, in their excellent book, *Stalking Trout,* outline principles for successful release.

These are:

● The use of the strongest practical nylon tippets to facilitate quick landing of fish. Long playing leads to metabolites such as lactic acid building up in the muscles and this kills fish.

● The use of a wide-mouthed net to minimise handling.

● The use of barbless hooks. These are difficult to obtain but can easily be 'adapted'. This does not lead to fish getting away, as one might expect.

● The use of artery forceps or slim-jawed pliers for removing hooks.

● Care in handling fish; wet the hands first, avoid the gill area, do not squeeze the stomach, and take care not to rub off scales.

Recently, I spent time with an enthusiastic Canadian angler who is a regular visitor to New Zealand. He lives in Alberta on the edge of the Banff National Park and fishes remote streams that few others reach. He has a 'pet' 2 kg brown trout that he has caught and released five times. On landing this fish for the first time, he clipped the adipose fin so he could recognise 'George'.

Anglers can help local acclimatisation societies and the Department of Conservation by weighing and measuring all trout caught, and supplying details from their diaries at the end of each season. This is especially important for fish that have been marked or tagged. Tags should be returned, along with the measurements to the Department of Conservation or to local acclimatisation societies. Metal or plastic tags are usually attached to the dorsal fin. Fish can also be marked by fin clipping or even removal. To determine right or left, look down on the fish's back with the head facing away from you. Always measure from the fork of the tail to the tip of the snout. Send details of species, weight, length and time and area of capture. Anglers' cooperation is vital in managing a fishery.

I think that more back country areas should be set aside as true wilderness zones, where helicopters are prohibited. A challenge would still be left for those anglers keen and fit enough to seek out trophy fish. Helicopters have their place and I have used them to my advantage in the past, but it can be depressing to have a machine land upstream from where you are fishing after you have spent three days tramping in to this so-called isolated spot.

Anglers must extend courtesy to landowners. Few farmers will deny access to fishing water provided permission is sought first. Please shut gates, avoid disturbing stock and offer thanks on the way out. Remember, the cost of fishing in many countries is well out of the reach of most anglers. Fortunately, we have not yet reached that stage, but treat landowners with respect so access for others will not be denied.

Finally, a comment about fishing etiquette. One winter morning my friend Dick and I were determined to be first to reach the Whitikau Pool on the Tongariro River. Unfortunately, although we arrived at dawn, another angler was first in the pool. This fisherman began upstream fishing at the tail of the pool, so Dick and I sat shivering patiently on the frosty bank waiting to start behind him. After 10 minutes, he had not moved one step upstream so I walked into the rapids below him and waited another 10 minutes. Finally, I asked him if he would mind moving upstream a little so my friend and I could start fishing. 'Look', he said, 'I got here first and you were second. I'm going to fish every inch of water in this pool even if it takes me all day.'

Finally he decided to move up a little. A confrontation on the river is entirely unnecessary and always detracts from the pleasures of angling. Usually, if another angler offends against our ideals of fishing courtesy it is through inexperience or excitement. A gentle word may be all that is necessary. If anglers are already fishing a pool you may join in but not in the water someone is just about to fish. If the pool is being fished downstream, start upstream of those already fishing. If they are fishing upstream, start downstream. Never start fishing a pool downstream when someone is already fishing upstream or vice versa. If in doubt, ask the angler fishing where you might start so as not to disturb the water. It is only common courtesy.

If your neighbour hooks a fish, leave plenty of room and reel in if required. Never fill a gap left by an angler landing a fish. This also applies to stream mouths. Join a line of anglers on the end unless there is a large gap. Even then, ask permission from the others before entering. Try not to disturb other anglers' water by excessive wading or walking close to the river bank. Finally, watch your back-cast and do not impede others by straying within casting range.

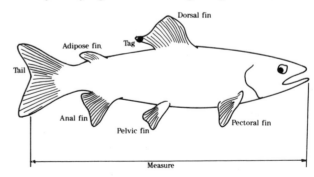

13

ACCLIMATISATION SOCIETIES
1. Mangonui — Whangaroa
2. Bay of Islands
3. Whangarei
4. Hobson
5. Auckland
6. Tauranga
7. Rotorua
8. Taupo
9. Taranaki
10. Stratford
11. Hawera
12. Waimarino
13. Wanganui
14. Hawke's Bay
15. Wellington

LICENCES
Three licences are required to fish the North Island
1. Taupo
2. Rotorua
3. Any other licence, apart from Southern Lakes, covers all other districts.

Northland

Generally, Northland waters become too warm in summer to sustain trout. However, there are a few exceptions, and some 15 streams hold a small population of trout. Only a few of these can be recommended, however.

Season   Open season 1 October — 30 September.

Waipapa River

This stream remains cool in summer under a canopy of trees. It fishes best in the cooler months, and contains rainbow in the 0.5–1 kg range which respond to a dry fly or nymph. Fish can be spotted in the brownish bush water. There are 10 km of fishable water upstream from the campsite. There are good deep holding pools and the river is easy to wade and pleasant to fish.

Location   This stream rises in the Puketi Forest, inland from Kerikeri and joins the Waihou River which empties into the Hokianga Harbour.

Access   Turn right off S.H.1 9 km north of Okaihau onto the Puketi Forest Pools Reserve road. There is an excellent campsite and picnic area on the banks of the Waipapa River.

Waiotu Stream and Kaimamaku Stream

Both contain a small population of rainbow in the 0.5–1 kg range. Fishing is best in the cooler months. Both streams cross farmland. There are few obstacles along the banks to impede casting.

Location   These two small feeder streams of the Wairua River, cross S.H.1 10 km north of Hikurangi and drain the Hikurangi Swamp. The Wairua flows in a south-westerly direction to discharge into the Kaipara Harbour south of Dargaville.

Access   Branch roads running north-east off S.H.1 near Otonga and Whakapara.

Kaihu River

Contains a small population of self-sustaining rainbow and brown trout in the 0.5–1 kg range. Not heavily fished.

Location   Rises in the Tutamoe Range, flows close to the Trounson Kauri Park and meets S.H.12 at Kaihu. It then flows south, parallel to, but east of, S.H.12 to join the Wairoa River at Dargaville.

Access   Turn off S.H.12 north of Kaihu on the road to Trounson Kauri Park. The river can be seen on your right, at first crossing farmland but soon entering a gorge.

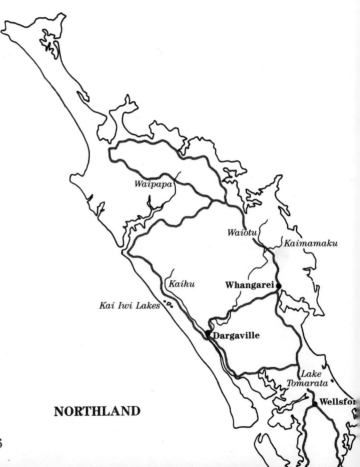

NORTHLAND

KAI IWI LAKES

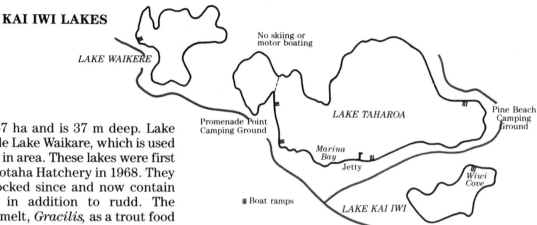

LAKE WAIKERE

No skiing or
motor boating

LAKE TAHAROA

Pine Beach
Camping
Ground

Promenade Point
Camping Ground

Marina
Bay

Jetty

Wiwi
Cove

▥ Boat ramps

LAKE KAI IWI

To Dargaville

Kai Iwi Lakes

Lake Taharoa covers 237 ha and is 37 m deep. Lake Kai Iwi covers 33 ha while Lake Waikare, which is used for water-skiing, is 35 ha in area. These lakes were first stocked from the Ngongotaha Hatchery in 1968. They have been regularly stocked since and now contain rainbow up to 4 kg, in addition to rudd. The introduction of a small smelt, *Gracilis*, as a trout food has been most successful. Koura, freshwater snails, bloodworms, freshwater crabs and mussels are also found. Lake Taharoa is the most productive lake although there is also good fishing in Lake Kai Iwi. The bag limit is 10 trout and the minimum size is 25 cm. Trolling and spinning are permitted although lure fishing from the shore accounts for most catches. Use a medium sinking line and caste over the blue line or shelf. Wading is safe. Recommended flies during the day include Parson's Glory, Muddler Minnow, Killer Patterns, Red Setter and Orange Rabbit. At night, try the usual black flies. Fishing is better in the cooler months of the year.

Location These three sand dune lakes lie 35 km north-west of Dargaville off S.H.12. There are two camping grounds, at Pine Beach and Promenade Point.

Access Turn off at Omamari Road, travel 11 km to the Kai Iwi Lakes Road, which leads to the Taharoa Domain.

Lake Tomarata

One side of the lake is weedy, but the other can be fished from the shore although a small boat is an advantage. Contains small rainbow trout.

Location   This lake covers 20 ha and lies between Wellsford and Mangawhai. The lake is north-east of Tomarata almost on the coast.

Access   Turn off S.H.1 at Wellsford on the Mangawhai Road. Travel 13 km and turn off to Tomarata.

Kerikeri

The Kerikeri irrigation dam has been stocked with rainbow and has been fishing well recently, according to local reports. It is an ideal place for junior anglers to start trout fishing. The Kerikeri Stream also holds small rainbow.

The Auckland Acclimatisation District covers a large area, from Helensville in the north to Taumarunui in the south. Also included are the Coromandel Peninsula and the fertile farmland around Matamata and Putaruru. For ease of description, the district is discussed under Auckland, the Waipa River system, the Waihou River system and the King Country.

Auckland

There are numerous small lakes in the Auckland area, many of which contain coarse fish. Only those holding trout will be described in any detail. There is an open season on all lakes from 1 October to 30 September.

Lake Ototoa

The Auckland Acclimatisation Society has regularly stocked this lake with rainbow trout. A trout weighing 3.5 kg was caught in the 1950s, and fish up to 2 kg are not unusual. The forestry or west side of the lake provides the best fishing with either a sinking line and a lure or a sink tip line and a nymph. Retrieve both slowly over the blue line. This lake also contains tench and rudd.

Location   Lies 30 km north-west of Helensville near the Woodhill Forest.

Access   Public road.

The remaining lakes in the Woodhill region — Kuwakatai, Kerata, Karaka, Piripoua, Pautoa and Ngaharu — all hold course fish. Other lakes containing course fish include Okaihou (Houghton's) at Muriwai, Wainamu at Bethells and Puketi at Waiuku. Parkinson's Lake near Otaua is closed. Pupuke, on the North Shore, holds small rainbow as well as coarse fish.

19

Lake Whatihua (Thompson's Lake)

The lake is easy to wade and rainbow up to 1.7 kg in good condition have been caught. A fish weighing 2.2 kg was landed in 1988.

Location　This small lake covers a little over 5 ha and lies 6 km south-west of Waiuku on the Waiuku–Karioitahi road.

Lake Otamatearoa (Muir's Lake)

Covers 7 ha and is surrounded by the Whiriwhiri race track. A boat is required as the lake margins are weed infested. Rainbow trout and tench are present in the lake.

Location　South-west of Waiuku at Whiriwhiri.

Access　Single access to fish and launch a small boat.

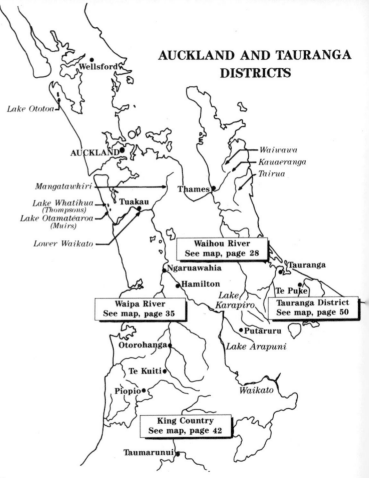

AUCKLAND AND TAURANGA DISTRICTS

Wellsford
Lake Ototoa
AUCKLAND
Mangatawhiri
Lake Whatihua (Thompsons)
Lake Otamatearoa (Muirs)
Lower Waikato
Tuakau
Thames
Waiwawa
Kauaeranga
Tairua
Waihou River See map, page 28
Tauranga
Ngaruawahia
Hamilton
Te Puke
Lake Karapiro
Tauranga District See map, page 50
Waipa River See map, page 35
Putaruru
Otorohanga
Lake Arapuni
Te Kuiti
Waikato
Piopio
King Country See map, page 42
Taumarunui

Auckland streams and rivers

A number of streams near Auckland offered reasonable fishing some years ago, but unfortunately they have deteriorated for a variety of reasons. These streams include the Wairoa near Hunua, the Mangatawhiri and the Mangatangi, all of which contribute to Auckland's water supply. The Mangawara, near Te Hoe north-east of Huntly, can fish quite well where it joins the Waikato River at Taupiri, but it is invariably silt laden.

Two streams on the Coromandel Peninsula hold stocks of small rainbow trout but are best fished in the cooler months of the year.

Season   1 October — 30 April, unless otherwise stated.

Waiwawa River

A pleasant small fly stream not holding large stocks.

Location   This river flows north and drains into the Whitianga Harbour.

Access   A small road follows upstream from Coroglen on the true right bank.

Tairua River

Fly fishing only in this river. Contains small rainbow. There are some deep holding pools and in favourable conditions an evening rise occurs. The river is used for rafting in summer.

Location   Drains the bush-covered Coromandel Ranges, flows in a northerly direction and empties into the top end of the Tairua Harbour.

Access   A small road from Hikuai follows upstream for some distance on the true right bank.

Lower Waikato River

This stretch of water includes that part of the river from the Karapiro Dam to the mouth at Port Waikato.

There is big, slow-flowing deep water in most places. The river is often willow infested and is not very scenic. However, the water quality has improved in recent years and the river now holds a reasonable stock of brown trout and a few rainbow. Most are resident fish although there are a few sea-run trout. In the autumn, a heavy spawning run occurs up the Waipa River at Ngaruawahia. Browns up to 3.5 kg have been caught mainly on spinning gear or on a deeply sunk lure. Night fishing using a Hairy Dog, Fuzzy-wuzzy, Craig's Night-time or a Black Phantom can be interesting. A red-bodied Hairy Dog will take fish during the day. Popular spots include just below the Karapiro Dam, at The Narrows between Cambridge and Hamilton, Cobham Bridge and Ferry Bank in Hamilton, Horotiu and on the wall at Huntly Power Station. An evening rise has been seen at the southern end of Kaiwaha Island and trout have been caught as far downstream as Otaua.

Location and access   Flows in a north-westerly direction through Cambridge, Hamilton and Ngaruawahia. It then bends north to Mercer and finally west to Port Waikato. It is not difficult to reach the river as it runs parallel to S.H.1 from Lake Karapiro to Mercer. A boat is a decided advantage on this river, and small boats can easily be launched at numerous spots.

Season   1 October — 30 September.

Lake Karapiro

A boat is necessary on this hydro lake as weed growth makes shoreline fishing very difficult. Fishing is best in the upper reaches and some shoreline angling is possible here. There are some large rainbow and brown trout above the Little Waipa confluence and at Salter's Flat where the water is heavy and fast. Early morning and evening are the best times to fish, whether trolling a spinner or fly casting from a boat.

Location   On S.H.1 between Cambridge and Tirau.

Access   Good access roads on both sides of the lake.

Season   1 October — 30 September. All legal lures and bait are permitted.

Lake Arapuni

All legal lures and bait are permitted. The lake is 35 km long but as with all the Waikato hydro lakes, weed growth has become a problem. This tends to obstruct the shore, but fishing is possible below the Waipapa Dam and from Bulmer's Road, Mangare Road, and Landing Road. Boat fishing is preferred, however. Both brown and rainbow can be caught trolling, harling or fly fishing from a boat. Early morning and evening are the best times to fish. Popular flies are green-bodied lures such as Green Orbit, Green Rabbit, Green Smelt and Green Maribou. After dark, try Hairy Dog and

Black Phantom. For the spin angler, try Black Toby and Cobra.

In June and July, worm fishing is popular off the Arapuni Dam. A specially constructed wire basket on a long pole is required to land fish.

Location   This hydro lake lies 16 km west of Putaruru.

Access   From the Putaruru–Arapuni highway.

Season   1 October — 30 September.

Boat launching   Options are: below the Waipapa Dam; Bulmer's Road; Landing Road, which leads to the Hamilton Anglers' Club lodge; Barnett's Road.

Mangawhio Stream

Above the falls, the river flows in a steep sided gorge and is difficult to reach. Fishing tends to be better in winter when good fish can be taken from the pools below the falls. Try a Red Setter or an Orange Rabbit on a sinking line.

Location   Rises near Ngaroma and enters the top end of Arapuni Lake.

Season   Above the falls from 1 October — 30 April; below the falls from 1 October — 30 Sept.

Access   Either by boat or by way of a bush track on the true left bank below the Waipapa Dam from a boat ramp. This leads to the falls.

Lake Waipapa

Local anglers maintain that fish are heavier from this lake because they contain mercury, which leaches into the lake from the Kinleith pulp mill. Despite this, Waipapa is the best of the hydro lakes from an angler's point of view. As with all these lakes, eutrophication has resulted in significant weed growth, so shoreline fishing is limited. Both rainbow and brown trout are present in sizes up to 3 kg. The Tokoroa Chicken is the favoured lure, whether trolled behind a boat or cast from the shore. Other lures and spinners are also successful provided they are fished deeply.

The Waipapa River below the falls is a favoured spot; use a high-density fly line and a luminous green-bodied lure and fish deeply across the current. Spinning is equally effective.

Waipapa River

This is an excellent fly stream, holding rainbow up to 2 kg. Wading can be tricky in parts due to deep slots in the rocky bed. Best fished in boots and shorts. The upper reaches are overgrown in places but, as is usually the case, they hold the largest fish. Try Hair and Copper, Hare's Ear, Half Back and Caddis nymphs, Coch-y-bondhu and Greenwell's Glory dry flies. A downstream sunk Red Setter or Hamill's Killer will also take fish, but this stream should really be fished with an upstream nymph. For the adventurous angler, there is plenty of water to explore in the bush.

I have visited this stream on a number of occasions and camped out with family members. My son, when he was 14 years old, claimed he hooked a large fish in a deep gut on a Red Setter. I have no way of proving this story as I was upstream at the time but he returned with a partially straightened hook and was quite convinced the fish and not a rock had been responsible.

Pokaiwhenua River

Unfortunately, this river has been affected by the Kinleith pulp and paper mills, and water flows have been reduced. The river flows over a bed of rock gravel and pumice. Rainbows are present above the falls, rainbows and browns below. Both respond to dry flies and small nymphs.

Location   Rises from spring-fed streams in the Tokoroa area, flows in a northerly direction west of Putaruru and enters the Waikato River opposite Horahora.

Season   1 October — 30 April.

Access   The river is divided into two sections by falls near the Putaruru–Arapuni road. Above the falls, good water can be reached from the old Waotu road which branches south off the Putaruru–Arapuni road. The mouth can be fished from a boat. The Horahora road crosses near the mouth.

Location   Runs parallel to, but west of, the Pokaiwhenua River and enters the Waikato River 5 km upstream from the Pokaiwhenua mouth.

Access   From Waotu, Pearson's Road, Hodderville and the Putaruru-Arapuni road.

Season   1 October — 30 April. Fly fishing only on this stream.

Little Waipa Stream

Clear water flowing over rock, gravel and pumice often between banks of weed. Above Pearce's Falls, rainbow are present whereas below the falls there are both rainbow and brown trout. A landing net is advised because of the weed. Fish between 0.75 and 2 kg can be expected. Try March Brown, Greenwell's Glory and Twilight Beauty dry flies; and Pheasant Tail, Hare's Ear and Hare and Copper nymphs, all in the smaller sizes.

Waihou River and tributaries

Season Open season from 1 October to 30 September for the Waihou River, the Waimakariri Stream and the Ohinemuri River downstream from the Victoria Street bridge (i.e., the boundary between Waihi Borough and Ohinemuri County). Also the Waitawheta River below Franklin Road crossing. For all other tributaries, 1 October — 30 April.

Waihou River

This river drains the Mamaku Plateau and the Kaimai Range to empty into the Thames Estuary. It is supplied by numerous feeder streams, most of which hold trout in the cooler months of the year. During the hot summer months when water flows are reduced, fish tend to drop back to the main river. This river system runs for 150 km and, along the Waikato River and tributaries, is the most important fishery in the Auckland District. Both brown and rainbow trout are present and fish up to 3.5 kg have been caught, although the average weight is in the 0.5–1.5 kg range.

Lower reaches

These reaches are sluggish, heavily willowed and unattractive. However, some sizeable trout have been taken on spinning gear and wet fly or lure between Shaftsbury and Gordon. This stretch of water provides a great resource of fish, and even after floods fish stocks are rapidly replenished.

Location and access The river flows in a northerly direction from Matamata to Thames and is readily accessible east of Te Aroha, Waharoa and Matamata from Old Te Aroha Road and Manawaru Road.

Middle and upper reaches

This river generally flows sedately across farmland. The upper reaches hold good-sized fish but they present quite a challenge in very clear water. Try floating a small nymph downstream on a sinking line, or wait for the evening rise. Fish are easily spotted and just as easily frightened. Some good-sized fish are present in these reaches. There are some excellent pools off Leslie's Road, and upstream from S.H.5.

Location Flows in a northerly direction east of Putaruru, through Okoroire to Matamata.

Access Upper reaches from White's Road near Putaruru and Leslie's Road through private farmland (prior permission essential). Lower down, the river can be reached from the Tirau–Rotorua road (S.H.5), from Okoroire, from S.H.29 west of Te Poi and from the Tauranga–Matamata road.

Waihou feeder streams

These will be described in order from the mouth of the Waihou River to its source. As with the Waipa River, these small streams hold limited stocks of fish, so catch-and-release is strongly recommended.

Kauaeranga Stream

Fly fishing only in this stream.

The middle reaches are favoured but the trout population is not large. Best early in the season before the valley is inundated by trampers and swimmers. Pleasant water to fish, with trout averaging 0.5–1 kg. Use small weighted nymphs and dry flies. Try Coch-y-bondhu, Black Gnat, March Brown and Blue Dun dry flies, and Pheasant Tail, Black Nymph, Olive Nymph and Hare and Copper nymphs in sizes 12–16.

Location Rises in the Coromandel Ranges and flows into the tidal estuary of the Waihou just south of Thames.

Access From the Kauaeranga Valley road.

Puriri Stream

Very small stream best fished early in the season.

Location and access From the Thames–Paeroa highway (S.H.26) 12 km south of Thames.

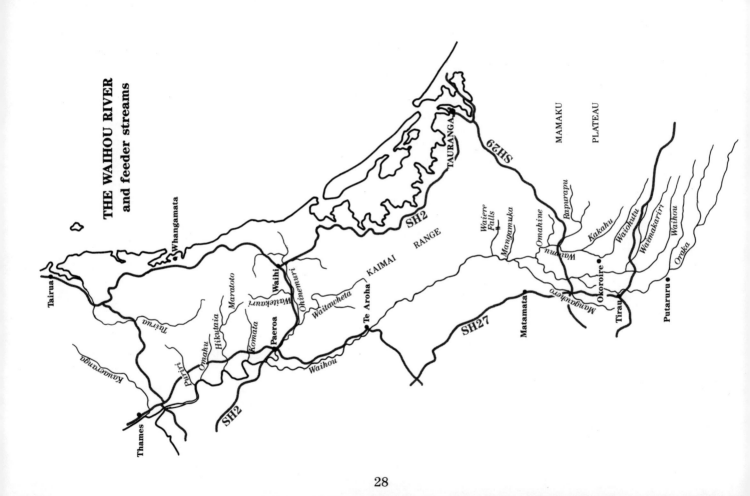

THE WAIHOU RIVER
and feeder streams

Whangamata

Tairua

Kauaeranga

Tairua

Thames

SH2

Puriri

Omahu

Hikutaia

Komata

Maratoto

Waitekauri

Paeroa

Waihi

Ohinemuri

Waitawheta

Te Aroha

Waihou

SH2

KAIMAI

RANGE

TAURANGA

SH29

MAMAKU

PLATEAU

Waiere
Falls

Mangamuka

Omahine

Waitawa

Rapurapu

Kakahu

Waiohutu

Waimakariri

Waihou

Oraka

Okoroire

Tirau

Putaruru

Mangauehero

Matamata

SH27

28

Omahu Stream

As for the Puriri Stream (above).

Location and access   From S.H.26 between Puriri and Hikutaia.

Maratoto-Hikutaia Stream

Fly fishing only in the Maratoto Stream and tributaries upstream from the old Whangamata Track.

Flows through farmland with a gravel and boulder bed. Overhung by willows in places but there are stretches of good clear nymph water and some stable holding pools.

Location and access   From S.H.26 at Hikutaia, then from the Hikutaia-Maratoto road. Good campsite in this valley. Access to Coromandel State Forest Park.

Komata Stream

Fly fishing only.

Small fly stream flowing through pasture and lined by willows. Holds rainbow in the 0.5–1 kg range. Fish it early in the season.

Location and access   From the Komata Valley road, off S.H.26 at Komata 6 km north of Paeroa.

Ohinemuri River

The open season below Victoria Street bridge.

During the Waihi goldrush, this river was polluted with cyanide used in gold recovery. Despite occasional severe floods, fish stocks recover rapidly and the river is rated highly by anglers. Holds equal numbers of brown and rainbow in the 0.5–1 kg range. The lower

---

Location   Rises from the southern slopes of the Coromandel Range and the northern slopes of the Kaimai Range. Traverses the picturesque Karangahake (Waikino) Gorge to join the Waihou at Paeroa.

Access   S.H.2 follows the river from Paeroa to Waihi.

---

reaches are best fished with a spinner or downstream smelt fly. There is a section of rough water in the gorge suitable for weighted nymphs. Above the gorge there are pools and runs lined by willows but fish are difficult to spot in the brownish water. Best fished in winter or early in the season.

Waitekauri Stream

Small feeder stream of the Ohinemuri best fished early and late in the season and containing both brown and rainbow trout averaging 0.5 kg.

Location and access Flows south in the Waitekauri Valley at Waikino.

Waitawheta River

Popular stream offering excellent fly water especially in the middle reaches. There are few fish in the gorge section and a small population in the upper reaches. Brown and rainbow trout respond to nymphs, dry flies and sunk lures such as Orange Rabbit and Hamill's Killer in the smaller sizes. Quite heavily fished and popular for picnics. Fish difficult to spot. Good camping at Dickies Flat. Some very deep holding pools.

Two other small streams, the Waimata near Waihi and the Hikurangi in the Athenree Gorge, hold fish but are not recommended.

Location Rises in the Kaimai Range west of Katikati. Flows in a northerly direction, leaves the bush and meanders across farmland to enter the Ohinemuri River downstream from Waikino.

Access From S.H.2 by crossing the Ohinemuri River at Waikino or from the Waihi-Waitawheta road, then from Franklin, Deans or Dickie's Flat Road. The Auckland Anglers' Club own a hut at the end of Deans Road.

Waiere Falls Stream

Small feeder stream holding a few fish early in the season. The Waiere Falls can be seen from S.H.27 near Waharoa. The early missionaries used this route when travelling from Hamilton to Tauranga. Water flows can be very low in dry summer conditions.

Location and Access From the Okauia road, east of Waharoa and Matamata.

Mangamuka Stream

Small spring-fed stream rising in the Kaimais holding small brown trout.

> **Location and access** Crosses the Okauia road (Old Te Aroha Road) 1 km north of the Crystal Hot Springs at Okauia.

Omahine Stream

Small fly stream which often remains clear when the Waiomu floods. Easy to wade.

> **Location and access** Crosses the Tauranga–Matamata road, just before joining the Waiomu River. Access off Omahine Road.

Waiomu River

Popular river holding mainly rainbow in 0.5–1 kg range. An occasional fish of 3 kg has been caught but the average weight of fish has fallen in recent years. There are 10 km of fishable water flowing over a shingle bed, and the river is easy to wade.

> **Location** Rises in Kaimais, flows in a north-westerly direction through pasture land to join the Waihou River north of Te Poi.
>
> **Access**
> ● The Tauranga–Matamata road crosses the river near Stopford's Road, 11 km from Matamata.
> ● The Tauranga–Hamilton highway (S.H.29) at Swaps Bridge east of Te Poi.
> ● From the Te Poi road, which runs parallel but west of the river.
> ● From Waiomu Road east of Okoroire.

Rapurapu Stream

Another small fly stream best fished early in the season when water flows are reasonable. Stocks not high. Fish drop back to the main river during reduced water flow in mid-summer.

> **Location and access** From Rapurapu Road which branches off the Tauranga–Matamata road, at the foot of the Kaimais.

Kakahi Stream

Fly fishing only in this small tributary of the Waiomu which is easy to wade.

Location and access   From Kakahi Road, linking Rapurapu Road with Waiomu Road.

Okara Stream

Holds a small fish population. The river has been polluted by the Tirau Dairy Factory in the past. Wet fly, nymph and spinning preferred in this stream. Overgrown in places and at least one local farmer uses the river as a dump.

Location   Rises near Tokoroa, flows north, east of Putaruru and Tirau, to join the Waihou just south of S.H.29 west of Te Poi.

Access   From Lake and Langland's Roads, off S.H.27 (Tirau–Matamata road).

Waimakariri Stream

Holds a large population of small rainbow and is a great learner stream. There are 12 km of fishable water on this popular stream suitable for spinning and fly fishing. The Auckland Acclimatisation Society had a hatchery on this river some years ago.

Location   Rises on the Mamaku Plateau east of Putaruru, flows in a westerly direction and joins the Waihou 3 km above the Okoroire Falls.

Access
● Crossed by the S.H.5 (Tirau–Rotorua highway) just west of Tapapa.
● Waimakariri Road follows upstream on the true left bank.

Season   Open season from 1 October — 30 September.

Waipa River and tributaries

Waipa River

Many of the small feeder streams flow through native bush and scrub in their upper reaches while the middle and lower reaches traverse farmland. The water tends to be brownish and trout are difficult to spot. A recent improvement in water quality has followed the closing of the shingle crusher at Otorohanga in October 1988.

Lower reaches   From Ngaruawahia to Pirongia the river is slow flowing, often silt laden and choked with willows. Despite this, some good fish have been taken on spinning gear. Both brown and rainbow trout are present and the odd fish up to 3.5 kg has been caught. There is a good spawning run up this river in the autumn from the Waikato River.

Middle reaches   From Pirongia to Otorohanga the river is still deep and willow lined but trout can be taken on lure, wet fly, dry fly and nymph, and on spinning gear. The river is clearer in this section.

Access off the Pirongia–Kawhia road, and the Otorohanga–Kawhia road (S.H.31).

Upper reaches   From Otorohanga to the headwaters offers the best fishing. There are 30 km of pools and runs over a gravel bed and while most of the river flows through farmland, there are patches of native bush along the banks. The most productive water is above Otewa where brown and rainbow up to 2 kg are not uncommon. Above Toa Bridge there is excellent fly fishing for at least 15 km, but there are very few fish above a landslide which occurred in 1985 and partially blocked the river. There is good water at the old Waipa Mill but fish stocks are sparse. The river is readily accessible from the Otorohanga–Otewa road. Roads in the vicinity of Rangitoto, east of Te Kuiti, also provide access, but permission should be sought before crossing private farmland. February and March are the most popular months as fish run into the upper reaches during this time. Favoured flies include Coch-y-bondhu, Lace-moth imitations and Twilight Beauty dry flies, while the old standby nymphs Pheasant Tail, Hair and Copper and Half Back are equally effective. Use the smaller sizes 12 and 14.

Location   Rises in the Rangitoto Range south of Te Kuiti, flows in a northerly direction close to Otorohanga and Pirongia to enter the lower Waikato River at Ngaruawahia.

Access   This will be described for each section of the river but generally the main river and its many tributaries are readily accessible.

Season   Downstream from Toa Bridge there is an open season 1 October — 30 September; above the bridge, 1 October — 30 April.

Waipa Tributaries

Season   1 October — 30 April. These are small feeder streams holding small stocks of fish. Catch-and-release methods are recommended.

Kaniwhaniwha Stream

This is a fly-fishing-only stream, very popular and heavily fished. The water is clear and fish can be spotted and stalked, although they tend to be very shy. Rainbows in the 0.5–1 kg range can be expected. The stream meanders through farmland with patches of native bush enhancing the scenic qualities. Popular for picnics and tramping access to Mt Pirongia.

Location   Flows off the northern slopes of Mt Pirongia and enters the Waipa north of Karamu.

Access   Turn off at Te Pahu on the Karamu Limeworks Loop road.

Mangauika Stream

Small fly stream flowing through farmland and holding limited stocks of small rainbow trout. Very pleasant to fish. Flows in summer can be reduced by the Te Awamutu Borough water supply draw-off from the upper reaches.

Location and access   Enters Waipa at Pirongia. Access from Mangauika and Hannings Roads.

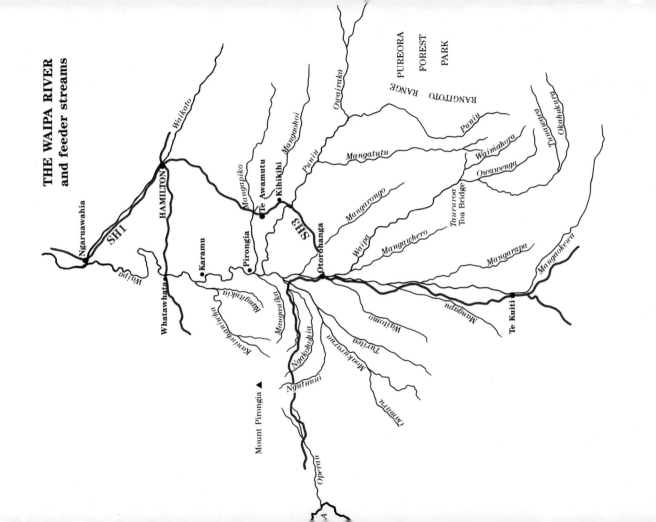

THE WAIPA RIVER and feeder streams

A typical Pirongia Stream, Waikato.

Ngakoaohia Stream

Holds both brown and rainbow trout in pools and runs over a rock and gravel bed.

Location and access   Flows east of Mt Pirongia. Access off the Pirongia–Kawhia road (S.H.31) and Pekanui Road, at Ngutunui. Fly fishing only in this stream from the source to the bridge on S.H.31.

Ngutunui Stream

Overhanging bush and high banks cause problems when fishing this small stream which holds both brown and rainbow in runs and pools.

Location and access   Flows off the southern slopes of Mt Pirongia and joins the Moakurarua Stream near S.H.31.

Moakurarua Stream

Offers 12 km of small stream fishing although the lower reaches are overgrown by willows. Holds mainly small rainbow. A tributary, the Oamaru, joins at the Honikiwi Road bridge and is also worth exploring.

Location   Flows north from Honikiwi to join the Waipa near Pirongia.

Access   From the Otorohanga–Honikiwi road, and then Turitea and Turoto Roads.

Turitea Stream

Not easy to fish, but there are some reasonable brown trout in pools beneath the willows.

Location and access   From S.H.31, which crosses east of the Moakurarua Stream and Turitea Road.

Waitomo Stream

Another small stream offering dry fly and small nymph water. There are some deep pools but the overgrown banks make fishing difficult on some stretches.

Location and access   From the Waitomo Valley road.

Mangapu Stream

Crosses the Waitomo Valley road, holds fish but is not recommended. Tends to be silt laden. Best at Oparure.

Mangaokewa Stream

Holds a reasonable stock of both brown and rainbow averaging 0.75 kg. Fish are hard to spot in the brown water. A pleasant river to fish, especially above the Mangaokewa Reserve on S.H.30.

> **Location and access** Flows north parallel to the railway line from Kopaki to Otorohanga and through the eastern suburbs of Te Kuiti.

Mangarapa Stream

Best in the upper reaches. Often silt laden further downstream.

> **Location and access** Flows north-west to join the Waipa just below Mangapu Junction. Can be reached from Hangatiki.

Waimahora Stream

Small stream best fished with a fly early in the season. Flows across farmland. Willow lined with a shingle bed.

> **Location and access** Enters the Waipa at Toa Bridge.

Mangatutu Stream

Very clear fly stream with few fish in the upper reaches above a sink hole. Best between Lethbridge Road and Wharepahunga. This stream is highly rated and a delight to fish.

> **Location** This is a large tributary of the Puniu which it joins near Waikeria.
>
> **Access** Off Wharepahunga Road and Lethbridge Road.
>
> **Season** 1 October — 30 April. Fly fishing only above Lethbridge Road bridge.

Puniu River

The Auckland Anglers' Club have a hut on Newman Road. There is excellent water in the middle and upper reaches but the lower reaches are not recommended. Fish can be spotted and both brown and rainbow average around 0.75 kg. The same flies as recommended for the Waipa are effective. A cautious approach is essential. The upper reaches flow through native bush and a good evening rise occurs in favourable conditions.

Location Rises in the Pureora Forest on the Rangitoto Range and flows from Wharepunga to join the Waipa at Pirongia.

Access
Upper reaches From the Kihikihi–Arapuni road, turn off at Bayley's Road, 5 km beyond the Orakau Battle site. Then from Newman and Wharepapa Roads.
Lower reaches S.H.3 crosses south of Kihikihi. Also from Tiki Road.

Season Below Wharepapa Road bridge, there is an open season 1 October — 30 September. Above the bridge, 1 October — 30 April. Above Bayley Road bridge the river is reserved for fly fishing.

Owairaka Stream

Has been described as a ditch overgrown with willows but some of these have recently been cleared. Flows through farmland over a shingle bed and although it holds fish the Puniu and Mangatutu are more highly rated.

Location and access Runs parallel to the Kihikihi–Mangakino road.

Mangahoi Stream

Small fly stream flowing through farmland and containing rainbows.

Location and access Flows from Pukeatua through Te Awamutu. Access off Parawera and Monkton Roads from the Kihikihi–Mangakino road.

Oparau River

Although the Oparau River drains Mt Pirongia it flows in a westerly direction to enter Kawhia Harbour. It is convenient to describe it in this section.

Delightful river giving access to a walking track up Mt Pirongia. However, it only holds small stocks of brown trout. Some sea-run fish enter the river late in the season.

Access From a loop road off S.H.31 linking Ngutunui with Oparau.

The area described in this section includes all that country lying between Te Kuiti in the north, Taumarunui in the south and the Tasman Sea in the west. Originally, dense native forest clothed these hills but now much of the bush has been burned and clear-felled to make way for pasture. The main river systems include the Awakino and Mokau rivers draining to the south-west, the Wanganui tributaries draining to the south, and around Te Kuiti, tributaries of the Waipa draining to the north and already described in the Auckland section. A New Zealand or Auckland licence covers this area and unless otherwise stated, the season opens on 1 October and closes on 30 April.

Marokopa River

Below the Marokopa Falls, the river is best suited to spinning. The lower 4 km are tidal and, along with whitebait, herrings and kahawai, an occasional sea-run brown trout is caught, not always by legal methods. Above the Falls, there are 8 km of good fly water, the river flowing through farmland but with scrub cover in places along the banks. Rainbow predominate in these reaches and fish average 1 kg. A sunk nymph fished upstream on a floating line is the most successful method.

Location Rises in the hills west of Waitomo Caves, flows on a westerly course through rugged limestone country and enters the Tasman Sea at Marokopa.

Access From the Waitomo Caves–Te Anga road leaves S.H.3 about 8 km south of Otorohanga.

Season Open 1 October — 30 September below the junction with the Mangatuahaua Stream. Above the junction, 1 October — 30 April.

Mangaohoe–Tawarau River

This river offers excellent fly water from above Mangaohoe all the way downstream to Te Anga. The river gorges in places, is partially bush lined and has deep stable pools and enticing runs. Fish can be spotted in the shallower runs but the water has a brownish tinge reducing visibility in deeper water. An energetic angler can walk the 16 km from Mangaohoe to Te Anga, but a night camped out is desirable. Boots and shorts are advised. Crossings can be somewhat tricky because of slippery stones. There are some very deep pools which provide good holding water in the lower reaches.

Location This tributary of the Marokopa rises near Waitanguru north-west of Piopio and flows in a northerly direction to enter the Marokopa at Te Anga. The upper reaches are known as the Mangaohoe, while the same river lower down becomes the Tawarau.

Access Mangaohoe — at Mangaohoe via Mangaotaki north-west of Piopio. Or Tawarau — from a short no-exit road running up the true left bank at Te Anga.

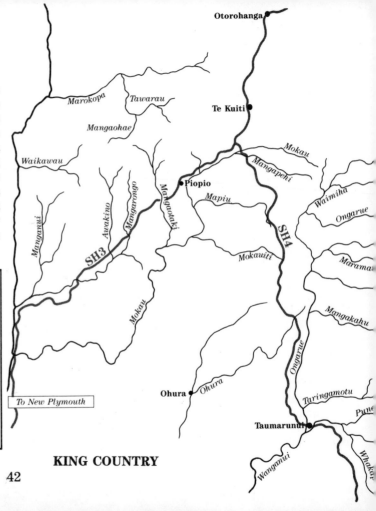

To New Plymouth

KING COUNTRY

42

Waikawau River

Small shingly stream flowing across farmland and holding only small stocks of trout. An occasional large sea-run brown trout has been caught, however. Not worth a special visit though the round trip from Marokopa to Awakino is recommended for the scenery.

> **Location and access**   This river enters the Tasman Sea mid-way between Awakino in the south and Marokopa in the north.

Awakino River and tributaries

Awakino River

Below Mahoenui, the river winds across farmland before entering the gorge. Because of its sluggish nature and tendency to become silt laden, the water is best suited to spinning. Both brown and rainbow are present, with fish up to 2 kg. Above Mahoenui, the river is a delight to fish, with clear pools and runs. The true left bank is bush covered and fish can be spotted and stalked. Try any small nymph or wet fly during the day and a Twilight Beauty or Coch-y-bondhu for the evening rise. Fish stocks had decreased at the time of writing, but hopefully this is a temporary phenomenon. Catch-and-release is strongly recommended. The fish are tricky to take during the day, accurate casting and fine gear being required.

> **Location**   Rises in the bush-clad Herangi Range west of Piopio, flows in a southerly direction to Mahoenui where it turns on a south-westerly course through the Awakino Gorge to reach the sea at Awakino.
>
> **Access**   *Middle and lower reaches* From S.H.3 between Awakino and Mahoenui.
> *Upper reaches* From Gribben's Road at Mahoenui, which follows upstream on the true right bank for 12 km.
>
> **Season**   Below the Mahoenui Bridge, there is an open season from 1 October to 30 September. Above the bridge, the river is reserved for fly fishing and the season closes on 30 April.

Manganui River

An important spawning stream for the Awakino, it holds limited stocks of small rainbow and brown trout. Is gorgey in places with some bush cover, but in the main is willow lined as it flows over farm land. Best fished early and late in the season.

> **Location**   Flows in a southerly direction to join the Awakino River just upstream from the mouth, at Awakino.
>
> **Access**   From the Waikawau road, which leaves S.H.3 just east of Awakino following the true right bank upstream.

Mangarongo Stream

This steam is definitely for the adventurous, active angler not frightened to lose half the fish hooked. Is gorgey, overgrown and very difficult to fish but holds good fish, as one would expect. Full of snags.

> **Location**   Flows in a southerly direction, parallel to, but east of, Gribben's Road at Mahoenui.
>
> **Access**   From the Mangarongo road, off S.H.3 about 4 km north of Mahoenui.

Mokau River and tributaries

Mokau River

The river does hold fish but is choked with weed as a result of eutrophication from fertiliser run-off and usually silt laden as a result of bank clearance. In summer, the water is slow flowing and warm. An evening rise occasionally occurs near Puketutu. Twenty years ago, good fishing was enjoyed on this river. Now it is only useful for eeling.

With the exception of the Mangaotaki River and the Mangapehi Stream, all other tributaries have suffered the same fate and are not recommended.

> **Location**   Flows on a south-westerly course parallel to but south of S.H.3 from Te Kuiti to the sea at Mokau.
>
> **Access**   The river can be reached off a number of roads but as the fishing is not recommended in the middle and lower reaches only access at Puketutu on S.H.30 should be noted.

Mangaotaki River

This is one of the most favoured rivers in the area. Below the S.H.3 bridge, the river runs in a gorge which can be fished down to the Mokau confluence but spinning is favoured in this stretch. Above S.H.3 there is excellent water holding brown and rainbow up to 1.5 kg. Fish are difficult to spot in the brownish water but there are some deep holes and interesting riffles. Patches of native bush enhance the scenic qualities of this popular river.

Location   Drains the Herangi Range west of Piopio and flows on a south-easterly course to join the Mokau River east of S.H.3 just north of Mahoenui.

Access   From the Piopio–Mangaotaki road, where it crosses the river 10 km west of Piopio at Battley's Bridge. Or from S.H.3 which crosses the river 10 km south of Piopio.

Season   Open season below Battley's Bridge from 1 October to 30 September. Above the bridge, 1 October to 30 April.

Mangapehi Stream

Rather sluggish brown stream crossing farmland and holding small rainbow. Not greatly fished.

Location and access   Rises east of Benneydale and flows in a westerly direction to join the Mokau south of Te Kuiti. Follows S.H.30 from Benneydale to Kopaki.

Wanganui tributaries north of Taumarunui

A number of excellent rivers drain the Pureora Forest Park and Hauhungaroa Range north of Taumarunui. These join the Ongarue River which enters the Wanganui River at Taumarunui. Fish are difficult to spot in these tributaries as the water has that brownish colour typical in streams draining bush-clad hills. All hold brown and rainbow trout, and fish up to 3 kg are not unusual especially in the headwaters of these rock and stone rivers.

Waimiha Stream

A highly recommended stream holding good stocks of trout, it is a delight to fish. The upper reaches are deep and slow flowing but hold big brownies sure to frustrate the most careful fly fisher. Try them at dusk on a Twilight Beauty, as in my experience this is the only way to catch them. The middle and lower reaches are willow lined in places, but access is excellent with superb water to fish. On a recent visit, to my disgust I found the rotting carcasses of 15 sheep had been dumped in the upper reaches. This hardly improved the water quality!

Location   Rises just south of Barryville on S.H.30 and flows in a south-westerly direction through bush-cleared farmland to join the Ongarue at Waimiha south of Benneydale.

Access   *Upper reaches* From S.H.30 across private farmland behind a Maori pa 10 km east of Benneydale.
Middle and lower reaches From the Waimiha Valley road, just north of Waimiha which runs east off the Waimiha–Mangapehi road. This runs alongside the stream.

Ongarue River

Willow lined in the middle and lower reaches, very similar to the Waimiha but holds slightly more water. Excellent fly water off Ongarue Stream Road and there is usually a good evening rise. The Okauaka tributary also holds rainbow. Highly recommended in the middle reaches. The lower reaches alongside S.H.4 are sluggish, often silt laden and hold few fish.

Location   Runs parallel to, but just south of, the Waimiha Stream.

Access   From the Ongarue Stream road, just north of Waimiha through private farmland.

Maramataha River

For the energetic angler who can deal with dense manuka scrub, deep pools and gorges. Certainly holds trout but is very difficult to fish. You are not likely to be disturbed by other anglers on this stream! The Waione Stream a little further south also holds trout.

Location   Flows in a westerly direction parallel to, but south of, the Ongarue Valley road.

Access   Waione Road, branching off the Ongarue Valley road, crosses this river.

Mangakahu Stream

Similar stream to those described but access is reasonable.

> **Location** Runs parallel to the tributaries described but further south.
>
> **Access** From the Mangakaha road, running east from Ongarue.

Pungapunga Stream

Also holds fish and can be reached from Taumarunui off S.H.41. Turn off to Ngapuke. Flows across farmland and has a shingle bed. Best fished early in the season, as the water becomes warm during summer.

Ohura River

Winds across farmland, but below Ohura the river is more suited to spinning. There are some reaches below Matiere that offer fly fishing. Rainbow predominate. Not highly rated. Choked with willows in places and rather sluggish brown water. Holds plenty of eels.

> **Location** Rises just north-west of Ongarue, flows in a southerly direction and joins the Wanganui River south of Ohura.
>
> **Access** Turn off S.H.4 on to S.H.40 at Mangatupoto about 20 km north of Taumarunui. This road to Ohura follows the river.

The other Wanganui River tributaries are described in the Waimarino District.

Tauranga District

The most important river system in this district is the Wairoa. Its many feeder streams drain the heavily bush-clad Kaimai Range. The main river enters Tauranga Harbour near Bethlehem and is tidal in the lower reaches. Unfortunately, the river and its tributaries have been considerably modified for hydro-electric power generation. There are 5 powerhouses operating on the Wairoa River system and 13 tributaries have been dammed or diverted. In 1981 the Ruahihi Canal collapsed, sending tonnes of rubble and mud into the river. Other smaller streams have reduced water flows as a result of draw-off for orchard irrigation. However, there is still some interesting water to explore.

> **Season** In all waters, 1 October — 30 June.

Tuapiro Stream

Holds small rainbow. Overgrown in places. Wet fly and nymph fishing are preferred by local anglers. The stream is used extensively for swimming in the warmer summer months.

> **Location and access** Enters the top end of Tauranga Harbour at Tanner's Point. Can be reached from MacMillan's and Woodland Roads, off S.H.2 north of Katikati.

Wairoa River and tributaries
Ohourere (Minden) Stream

Falls prevent fish running up from the Wairoa. Use dry flies and small nymphs. Fish average 0.5 kg, and the catch rate is not high. However, the stream is pleasant to fish, easy to wade and popular for picnics.

Fly fishing only in this stream.

Location and access   Small stream rising in the Kaimais behind Te Puna. Can be reached from Wairoa Road, off S.H.2 at the main Wairoa River bridge. Follow onto Crawford's Road which meets the stream at a picnic area.

Opuiaki Stream

Reduced water flows have seriously affected this stream, which holds both brown and rainbows. Fish can be spotted and stalked with a dry fly or nymph.

The Mangapapa Stream entering the top of McLaren's Lake has been affected by hydro development. The Ngatuhoa Stream above the falls at Ngatuhoa Lodge also holds fish, but is not recommended due to access being difficult.

Location and access   From Soldiers Road, off S.H.29 just beyond the Ngamuwahine Bridge. Soldiers Road crosses the stream on a low level concrete bridge.

Ngamuwahine Stream

Delightful picnic area with native bush bordering the stream. Contains small rainbow and brown trout but the fish population is not high. Best fished with an upstream nymph. Fish are not easy to spot in the brownish bush water of the middle and upper reaches.

Location and access   Flows in an easterly direction from behind Whakamarama to join other streams east of S.H.29 (Tauranga–Hamilton highway) and enters McLaren's Falls Lake. Reached from S.H.29 which crosses the stream 15 km out of Tauranga. A small unsealed road follows upstream on the true right bank to a private farm.

Te Ahuru Stream

Small fly stream joining the Ngamuwahine near the S.H.29 bridge. Contains small brown and rainbow trout.

Omanawa River

Not an easy river to fish; boots and shorts recommended. Contains mainly rainbow up to 1.5 kg, and these can be taken on a nymph, sunk lure or spinner. There are fish above the Omanawa Power Station but this section is not highly regarded.

> **Location and access** Flows parallel to, but east of, Omanawa Road, from the Omanawa power station, to enter the Wairoa below the Ruahihi power station. Access across private farmland is often very difficult due to a deep gorge.

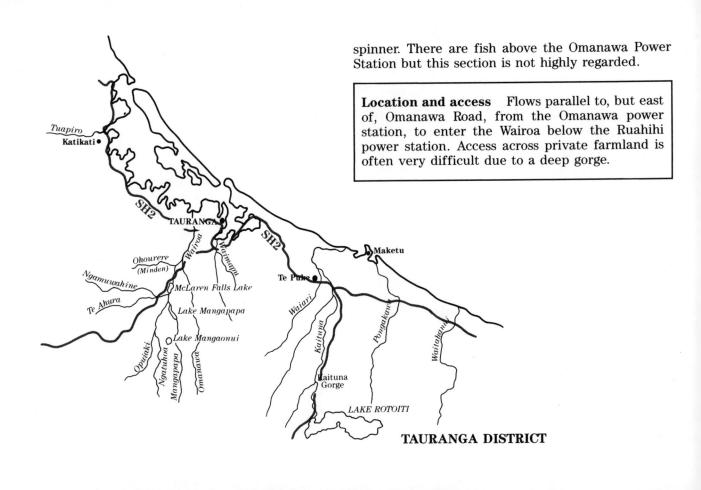

TAURANGA DISTRICT

Wairoa River

There is very little water to fish due to fluctuating water flows and difficult terrain below the McLaren's Falls power station. An occasional good fish has been taken below the Ruahihi power station on a smelt fly early in the season, when trout are chasing whitebait.

> **Location and access** S.H.29 follows and crosses the river 10 km from Tauranga. The lower reaches are crossed by S.H.2 but the river is sluggish and tidal at this level.

McLaren's Lake

Holds limited stocks of brown and rainbow but is easier to fish from a dinghy or with a spinner. The shoreline is rather muddy and difficult to wade. The Park is a great picnic spot, containing many fine specimen trees.

> **Location and access** Off S.H.29 on McLaren's Falls Road, to McLaren's Falls Park.

The hydro waters of the upper Opuiaki and Mangapapa Rivers which form Lakes Mangaonui and Mangapapa all contain fish. Of the Wairoa system, the 'unmodified' Ngamuwahine River would be my first choice to visit, not so much for the catch rate, but for the solitude and scenic qualities.

Waiari Stream

Small slow-flowing stream holding limited stocks of small brown and rainbow trout. Mainly fished with spinners and wet flies.

> **Location and access** Flows in a northerly direction to enter the Kaituna River north of Te Puke. Can be reached off No. 1 Road or Te Matai Road through private land, and from S.H.2 which crosses east of Te Puke.

Kaituna River

See Rotorua District for upper reaches.

Deep, slow-fishing river not very attractive to fish. Holds brown and rainbows averaging 0.75 kg. Early in the season, whitebait enter the river, so smelt flies, silver spinners and live bait account for most of the fish taken. Kahawai enter the mouth and the occasional sea-run rainbow has also been caught. Inanga can be used in this river.

Location   Six km below the outlet of Lake Rotoiti, the river enters an inaccessible gorge for 20 km. It emerges to flow sedately through farmland, becomes tidal and sluggish in the lower reaches and enters the sea near Maketu.

Access   The gorge area is virtually impossible to reach. Below the gorge the river can be reached through private farmland off Maungarangi Road, Rangiuru Road, S.H.2 east of Te Puke and the Kaituna River road.

Waimapu Stream

Limited stretch of dry fly and nymph water holding small brown trout in good condition. Quite highly regarded by anglers living in the district. Local knowledge an advantage.

Location and access   Rises in the hills behind Oropi, flows in a northerly direction and enters the Waimapu Estuary of Tauranga Harbour near Greerton. Can be reached off Oropi Road through farmland.

Pongakawa Stream

Middle reaches hold small rainbow and can be fished with spinner's wet flies or inanga live bait.

Location and access   Small spring-fed stream which crosses S.H.2 near Pukehina east of Te Puke. Reached from S.H.2, Benner's Road and Rotoehu Road.

Waitahanui Stream

Contains limited stocks of small rainbow.

Location and access   Drains from the Rotoehu Forest and flows down the Otamarakau Valley. Reached from Otamarakau Valley Road.

It is thought the Rotorua area was first settled about the middle of the fourteenth century by Maori from the Arawa Canoe. Hans Tapsell from Maketu was the first European to visit Rotorua about 1830, followed by the missionary Thomas Chapman in 1831. The area is world famous for its thermal activities and is well serviced with hotels and motels.

As can be seen from the Acclimatisation Societies' district map, the Rotorua District includes areas away from Rotorua, but this section deals with the dozen or so lakes within half an hour's drive of the city. Most of these lakes offer shoreline fishing, but a boat is a decided advantage and opens up areas that cannot be reached by road. All lakes contain rainbow trout and also some brown trout, but these are generally in the minority and more difficult to catch.

Lake Rotorua

The lake covers 7878 ha and is relatively shallow, being 25 m deep in the deepest part. Apart from the built-up areas, the lake is surrounded by farmland. There have been pollution problems and in summer when the lake warms up, blue-green algae have been troublesome. The shoreline is safe to wade and there are good access roads all round the lake. Rainbows average 1–1.5 kg, brown trout 3 kg.

Fly fishing from the shore Stream mouths are favoured locations, especially after dark. When the lake temperature rises in summer, trout congregate in large numbers in the cooler water, and the fishing can be excellent from late December through to March. Then in April, trout begin their spawning runs, and though fish can be taken they do not congregate prior to running. Stream mouths are all shallow, so trout remain wary during the day unless the lake is ruffled by a stiff breeze. Fishing is best with an off-shore breeze. Use a sink tip, floating or slow-sinking line.

Recommended lures to use during the day are smelt patterns, Dorothy, Hamill's Killer, Killwell No.1, Lord's Killer and Leslie's Lure. At night, use Craig's Night-time, Fuzzywuzzy, Hairy Dog, Maribou patterns and Hamill's Killer.

Brown trout can also be stalked along the shore during the day. Try wading out some distance and looking back into the shallows through polaroid glasses. Large browns can often be seen. Cast well ahead of cruising fish and use a small (size 8–10) smelt fly or even a nymph. An elderly friend considered this type of fishing very exciting during January, February and March.

Spinning can be carried out from shore providing you are 300 m from any stream mouth.

Fly casting at stream mouths is permitted from an anchored boat and can be most rewarding when the lake is warm.

Stream mouths
- Utuhina. Access from Arataua Street. There are some sunken logs and boulders at the mouth.
- Ngongotaha. Access from Beaumont's Road, or Taui Street along the beach. Best when the wind is from the west.
- Waiteti. From Arnold or Operina Streets. Shallow mouth; wading is possible for 200 m from shore.
- Awahou. Access from Gloucester Street. Considered the most productive mouth and is heavily fished in January and February. Best in west or north-west winds.

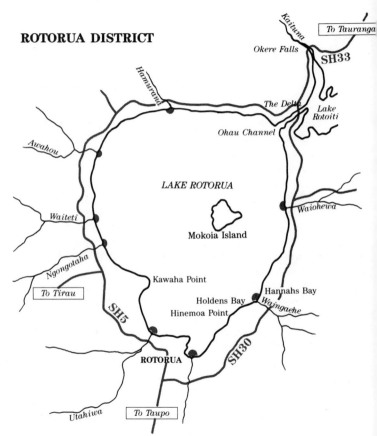

ROTORUA DISTRICT

• Hamurana Springs. There is no fishing upstream of the road bridge.

Other small streams include the Waiowhiro, Waikuta, Waiohewa and the Waingaehe (Holden's Bay Stream). These will only take 2 or 3 rods and fish best with an off-shore wind and floating line. Some need permission to reach through private property.

Trolling and harling Half the trout caught in Lake Rotorua are landed from boats. Trolling and harling is prohibited within 300 m of stream mouths. The most difficult period for trolling is during January, February and March when fish gather in the cooler waters around stream mouths. Fish can be caught anywhere in the lake, although round Mokoia Island is a favourite location. Other spots worth trying are off Kawaha Point, Sulphur Point and Hinemoa Point, the Airport Straight, Whakatane Turn-off and the Ohau Channel. Early morning or late afternoon are the most productive times. When harling a fly, use a high density fly line; lead or wire lines are not permitted. The same flies as listed for stream mouths can be used for trolling with the addition of Ginger Mick, Parson's Glory and Mrs Simpson.

When trolling a spinner try a Cobra, Billy Hill, Toby or a Flatfish. Blue, black and green are favoured.

Lake Rotorua can be treacherous in bad weather so keep an eye on the sky and the wind.

Location Rotorua City lies on the southern shore.

Season There is an open season on this lake from 1 October — 30 September. For the streams flowing into the lake the season is from 1 December — 30 June.

Boat ramps There are seven — situated at Hamurana (2), Ngongotaha (2), Rotorua City (2), and Hannah's Bay (see map). The ramps at the Soundshell, Motutara Point, Hannah's Bay, Hamurana, Ward Road (Hamurana), and Reeme St (Ngongotaha), are concrete.

Rotorua Streams

Only the Utuhina, Ngongotaha and Waiteti are open for fishing 1 December — 30 May. In the early part of the season, recovering kelts can be taken on nymph and dry fly. However, the best fishing is later in the season during April and May when run fish are in good condition. These can be taken on a small nymph or traditional lure, but as the streams are small, often overgrown and clear, fishing is not easy. I recently met a young angler on the Waiteti successfully using a Glow Bug.

Ohau Channel

Fish live and spawn in the Channel and also migrate through at certain times of the year. The water is deep, and a fast-sinking line should be used. As there are few spawning areas in Rotoiti, many trout from this lake move through the Channel to spawn in the Rotorua streams. For this reason fishing tends to be good both early and late in the season so October — November and April — June are prime seasons.

During the day, try smelt patterns, including Hawk and Silver, Silver Dorothy, Yellow and Silver Rabbit, Ginger Mick and Jack Spratt. At night use the usual night patterns, especially Craig's Night-time.

The Delta

Wading can be tricky as the bottom is uneven. The lip is also deep and drops off suddenly. Stand back 10 m or so from the lip and fish over it using a sinking line and a slow retrieve. April, May and June are the best months. Few anglers fish here at night, perhaps because of difficulties in wading. Use the same flies as for the Channel with the addition of Hamill's Killer, Killwell No. 1 and Mrs Simpson.

Lake Rotoiti

Rotoiti is the third largest lake in the Rotorua area and covers 3340 ha. The northern shore is bush clad.

Few streams of significance enter this lake and most fishing is done from a boat. Fish can be taken any time from any place although the hot summer months are often hard. Recommended trolling areas include the northern bush-clad shore, Sulphur Bay, Pateko Island, Cherry Bay, Coles Bay and Te Arero Bay. Harling a fly on a high-density fly line is often more effective than trolling hardware. Try Parson's Glory, Orange Rabbit, Red Setter, Cobra, Billy Hill, Pearl or a Toby. Black is a popular colour.

Fly fishing From April to the end of October fly fishing can be good at a few small stream mouths. Use a floating, sink-tip or slow-sinking line and during the day try Parson's Glory, Killwell, Hamill's, Mrs Simpson or Jack Spratt. At night, try Hairy Dog, Scotch Poacher, Taihape Tickler, Black Phantom or Craig's Night-time. The most popular spot is at Ruato where the small Twin Streams empty into the lake. An off-shore wind is desirable. Fish can be caught off the beach using a floating line. Try from dusk and if the fishing is slow by 9.30 p.m., it is probably is not worth persisting. The main disturbance at Ruato are logging trucks which thunder along the main road behind you. However, some excellent rainbow, some up to 4.5 kg, have been taken here over recent years.

Other fly fishing spots are at Haupara Bay, Emery's Reef, Gisborne Point, Waiiti Stream (weed infested)

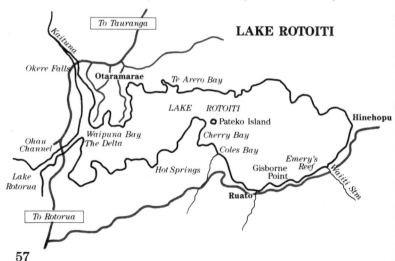

and the drains at Hinehopu. All these spots are open for winter fishing.

Spotting and stalking fish is very difficult during the day unless fish are actively smelting.

Two of my bridge-playing companions have had some success off the bush-clad shore near Hinehopu. Their technique is to tie their boat to an overhanging tree, cast a spinner out over the blue line, read the Sunday paper and then slowly retrieve.

Location   Lies east of Lake Rotorua and is connected by the Ohau Channel.

Access   S.H.30 follows the southern shoreline and S.H.33 the western shoreline.

Season   1 October — 30 June. In the winter season, 1 July — 30 September for shoreline anglers only from Rauto Bay to Hinehopu and the Kaituna River below Okere. No lead or wire lines are permitted.

Boat ramps   Otaramarae, Waipuna Bay, Gisborne Point and Hinehopu. All are concrete or bitumen except Waipuna which is pumice. Otaramarae is the deepest.

Kaituna River

Fish can be taken on dry flies, nymphs and lures. In the summer there is often a good evening rise. Rainbow average 0.75–1.5 kg and are generally in good condition.

Favoured dry flies include Twilight Beauty, Red Spinner, March Brown and Sedges. Use small lures and wet flies. Any size 12–14 nymph will take fish.

Location   Drains lake Rotoiti at Okere. (See Tauranga — Te Puke section for lower reaches.)

Access   From S.H.33. Turn off at Okere Falls; the road follows the true left bank to the Trout Pool. There are bridge and walking tracks downstream and stands have been constructed for anglers.

Season   There is an open season on this river below Okere Falls. Spinning is permitted.

Lake Tarawera

Tarawera has always been a dark, forbidding lake for me. It is very deep and dominated by the now-inactive volcano. Bush-clad hills surround most of the shoreline and in winter Tarawera can be cold and inhospitable.

The lake can cut up very rough during a strong southerly or even in an easterly; boat owners be warned. Despite this, Tarawera is renowned for its trophy rainbow which can be up to 6–7 kg in weight. They are not easy to catch, however.

Shoreline fishing Stream mouths are the top spots during April, May and June, but angling pressure can be intense. Some fish can be taken in the daytime, but most are caught in the evening, early morning and at night. Legal fishing time, as in the Taupo District, is from 5 a.m. to midnight irrespective of daylight saving. At the Te Wairoa Stream mouth, I have been fourth in line at 4.15 a.m. waiting to enter the water at 5 a.m.

Favoured lures include smelt and Rabbit patterns, Hamill's Killer, Killwell No. 1, Leslie's Lure and Parson's Glory, in sizes 6–8, while at night the usual night fly patterns are effective, especially those tied with luminous body material.

Te Wairoa Stream mouth — Follow the track to the right from the carpark at the Landing for 150 m to reach the mouth. Holds 5 to 6 rods but care is needed when wading as the drop-off is very deep. Stand back and fish quietly over the lip with a medium sinking line.

The Jetties — Use a sinking line off the jetties but a floater if fishing the tiny stream mouth to the left.

The Main Beach — During an easterly, anglers crowd this beach as schools of fish move close in to the stirred-up waves. Even if not fishing, the action can be quite amazing at times.

The Orchard — Walk to the left from the carpark beneath the rocky bluff to a small stream which empties into shallow water. Only holds 2 rods. False air casting with a floating line is recommended. Start well back as fish move close in early morning and at dusk.

Rangiuru Bay — Drive along Spencer Road to a picnic area and boat ramp by the willows. This bay is closed to trolling and fish can be taken by casting over the lip.

Waitangi Bay — A small stream enters through private property so access to this spot is by boat.

All the spots described above fish best in a westerly or south-westerly with the exception of the Main Beach.

The Outlet — This area is closed to fishing to preserve spawning.

The Waterfall — Enters Te Wairoa Bay beyond the Orchard and can only be fished by casting from an anchored boat.

Twin Streams — Access by boat between Te Wairoa and the Wairua Arm. Fly cast from an anchored boat or wade the shelf and fish over the lip.

Wairua Stream — Access is by boat to the head of the Wairua Arm. Very heavily fished in April, May and June, but can offer great fishing. It can be frustrating, especially during the day when the water literally turns pink from the great school of fish waiting off the stream mouth. Fishes better with 2 to 3 rods, but this is a rare event these days. Fly casting from a boat is not permitted within 15 m of the mouth. I have slept a number of nights curled up in a boat at this spot, to be kept awake after midnight by trout splashing their way up the stream. I have even heard a stag roar.

Location   Lies south-east of Rotorua.

Access   Turn right off the Whakatane highway at Ngapuna and drive 15 km past the Buried Village. The Outlet can be reached through the Tasman forestry from Kawerau; a permit is required from the forestry manager. However, the Outlet has recently been closed to fishing to allow spawning to be undisturbed.

Season   1 October — 30 June, except the Outlet which closes on 30 May. Wire and lead lines can be used, but as is usually the case, no trolling is permitted within 300 m of any stream mouth, nor within the confines of Rangiuru Bay. Apart from the Outlet, all other streams are closed to fishing.

Boat ramps   There are concrete ramps at the Landing and Stony Point Reserve, and pumice launching areas at Kariri Point Boatsheds, Otumutu and Te Tapahoro.

Trolling and harling — This can be very slow in the hot summer months and most fish are caught on lead or wire lines just off the blue line or shelf. Harling a size 4 Parson's or Yellow Rabbit on a high density fly line can be productive in October and November, especially in the early morning or evening. Favoured spinners include Flatfish, Toby, Cobra and the Zed Spinner. Fish can be taken anywhere and at any time providing one has the patience.

Lake Okataina

This beautiful deep lake is surrounded by native bush.

Has very limited shoreline fishing along the beach at Turanganui Bay (Home Bay). This is the only boat-launching area.

Fly fishing from an anchored boat   Use a high density line and the usual smelt or Rabbit patterns, Parson's Glory, Taupo Tiger or Killer patterns. Prime spots are stream mouths, the Log Pool, Te Koutu (Maori) Point, Parimata and Kaiakahi Bays. As is usual in Rotorua lakes, fish go deep during January, February and March.

Harling and trolling a fly or a spinner   The secret of success in this lake is to get down deep, so lead or wire lines or a length of such a line is necessary. Use the flies listed for fly casting and try spinners such as Toby, Flatfish, Cobra, Penny and Tasmanian Devil.

There are rainbows in excellent condition in this lake — up to 3 and 4 kg.

Location and access   Turn right at Ruato on S.H.30 and travel for 6 km along a scenic, bush-lined road.

Season   1 October — 30 June.

Lake Rotomahana

The world-famous Pink and White Terraces were sited on the shores of this lake before the Mt Tarawera eruption in 1886. There is still a considerable amount of thermal activity in this area with steam rising from cliffs. Rotomahana is an attractive lake, bush fringed and dominated by Mt Tarawera.

Fishes best during April, May and June. During May, no motors are permitted on this lake as it is a wildlife refuge during the duck-shooting season. Fly casting from an anchored boat, harling a fly or trolling can all be productive in the autumn and early winter. Try Mrs Simpson, Red Setter, Hamill's Killer and Killwell No. 1 in sizes 6–8. Rainbow up to 4 kg can be anticipated and these fish are in excellent condition and fight vigorously.

61

> **Location and access**   Turn off S.H.38 on the Rerewhakaaitu road, then take Ash Pit Road to Rotomahana. A boat is required to fish this lake and a dinghy can be launched from the end of the road although this spot is often rather muddy. There is a pleasant 1–2 hour walk through to this lake from Hot Water Beach on Lake Tarawera.

Lake Rotoehu

Contains only rainbow averaging 1–1.5 kg. Mainly fished from a boat using the methods described for the smaller lakes. There is limited stream-mouth fishing in the autumn in Te Pohue Bay. Use a floating line and black fly at night.

> **Location**   S.H.30 passes the southern shore of this shallow lake while the Pongakawa Road touches part of the eastern shore.
>
> **Season**   1 October — 30 June.
>
> **Boat-launching facilities**   There are no ramps but small boats can be launched off the beach at Te Pohue Bay, Kennedy's Bay and Otautu Bay.

Lake Rerewhakaaitu

Trolling, harling, spinning and fly casting will all take fish. A sinking fly line should be used. The favoured areas are Homestead Arm, Crater Bay, Ashpit Bay, Lone Pine and School Arm. This is a popular spot for camping in summer, but the best fishing occurs in the cooler autumn months. The usual flies and spinners as described for Lakes Rotorua and Rotoiti should be used. There is safe wading. Only rainbow are present.

> **Location**   Turn off S.H.38 approximately 5 km from Rainbow Mountain onto the Rerewhakaaitu road.
>
> **Season**   1 October — 30 June. No trolling is permitted inside the markers on Homestead Arm. Fishing is permitted from an anchored boat. No lead or wire lines allowed.
>
> **Boat-launching facilities**   There is a concrete ramp at Halfmoon Bay and boats can be launched from the shingle beach at Awaatua Bay.

Lake Okareka

This is a most attractive lake and a number of permanent residents commute daily from here to

Rotorua. Most of the lake is surrounded by farmland although there is an area of bush along the northern shore.

Generally fished from a boat; the most productive time is in the autumn. Use a high density fly line and a long trace with a Parson's Glory or a Red Setter. The Black Toby, Cobra and Flatfish take their share of fish. Favoured areas are the northern shore and the eastern end of the lake in May and June.

Location   Branch off the road to the Buried Village either just before or at the Blue Lake (Tikitapu).

Season   There is an open season on this lake.

Boat ramp   Concrete ramp at the south-western corner.

Lake Rotoma

This is a very deep, clear lake, often difficult to fish. Except for a recent introduction of 'tiger' fish (a sterile cross between a brook and a brown trout) all fish are rainbow. Most fishing is done from a boat either fly casting, harling a high density fly line, or trolling. In summer, a lead or wire line is necessary to reach fish.

The usual 'Rotorua' flies and spinners are successful.

Favoured spots are along Oneroa Beach in May and June when trout gather to spawn, Rotoiti Bay and along the western side of Tourist Point.

Location and access   Travel beyond Rotoehu on S.H.30 towards Whakatane. This road follows the southern shore. The Manawahe road parallels the northern shore.

Season   1 October — 30 June. Lead and wire lines are permitted.

Boat Ramps   Concrete ramps are situated at Otamatahei Bay, Whangaroa Bay and Merge Lodge.

Lake Tikitapu (Blue Lake)

Contains large numbers of small rainbow but fish up to 2.5 kg have been caught. An experimental hybrid, the zebra (rainbow-fontanalis cross), was released in 1984. Boat fishing is the usual method.

Three other small Rotorua lakes contain rainbow — Ngapouri, Ngahewa and Okaro. The first two are overstocked and the latter is used for water-skiing. Lake Rotokakahi (Green Lake) is privately owned and closed to fishing.

Location Tarawera Road follows the north-eastern shore.

Boat ramp The Rotorua Water Ski Club operates on this lake and two-thirds of the lake is for skiing only.

A 6.2 kg rainbow, Tongariro River, 1988.

64

Rangitaiki River System

This extensive and varied waterway lies in the Rotorua District.

Rangitaiki River

Upper reaches   South of S.H.5, access is very difficult as the banks are overgrown. Good fish can be caught on a spinner, however. North of S.H.5, there are 30 km of fishable water within the exotic forest. Low Level Road generally provides reasonable river access, and a camping ground offers basic facilities. Brown and rainbow trout up to 4 kg are present, and can be taken on a dry fly, nymph, downstream lure or spinner. There is often a good evening rise. The river is slow flowing in stretches but gorges and becomes difficult to fish 5 km above the junction with the Whaeo River. Fish are not easy to spot except in ideal bright conditions.

Middle reaches   The river is large and difficult to fish in the Murupara–Galatea–Matahina area as the banks are overgrown with willows. In the clear spots, good

Location   Rises on Lochinvar Station south of the Taupo–Napier road and flows in a northerly direction through the Kaiangaroa Forest and down through Murupara, Galatea, Matahina and Edgecumbe to enter the sea near Thornton.

Access   *Upper reaches*   From the Taupo–Napier road (S.H.5) at Rangitaiki or from the Kaiangaroa Forest off either S.H.5 or S.H.38. A permit is required to enter the forest. This can be obtained from the Forestry Corporation at Kaiangaroa or Murupara. A map of the forestry roads should also be purchased, as it is very easy to get lost.
Middle and lower reaches From the Murupara–Edgecumbe road.

Season   Open 1 October — 30 September below confluence with Otamatea Stream. Above this junction, 1 October — 30 June.

fly and spin fishing can be obtained usually by crossing private farms. A friend enjoys this section of river because of the solitude. There is a good rise on calm warm summer evenings.

Lower reaches   Below Matahina Dam there is a fast heavy water more suited to spinning and lure fishing.

There are two hydro lakes, Aniwhenua and Matahina, on the Rangitaiki River.

Lake Matahina

Contains browns and rainbows averaging 1–1.5 kg. Boat fishing, trolling a spinner, accounts for most fish caught, although fly and spin fishing from Lukes Road and at Clear Creek, at the western end of Waiohau Bridge, can be rewarding. Wading is safe.

This water has recently been disturbed by repairs to the earthquake-damaged earth dam.

Location   Lies a few kilometres south of Te Teko on the Murupara–Edgecumbe Road.

Access   From Rototaha Road on the eastern side of the lake.

Lake Aniwhenua

There are large, good-conditioned brown and rainbow trout in these waters, and fish up to 4 or 5 kg can be anticipated. It is easier to fish from a boat although there is some shoreline fishing. Fish can be taken trolling a spinner, harling a fly, spinning or nymphing from the shore, and night fishing using the usual large black fly. Fly casting from a drifting boat with a slow sinking line and a small wet fly or a floating line and a nymph are the best methods. Fish can occasionally be seen moving along the shore, but are not easy to spot and stalk. Because of the size and condition of fish caught, this lake is very popular. The lake tends to fish best from February to June.

Location   Formed in 1980, this shallow lake lies north of Galatea and the confluence of the Horomanga and Rangitaiki rivers.

Access   From the causeway on Kopuriki Road at the top of the lake, or from Eastern Access Road.

Season   1 October — 30 September.

Boat-launching facilities   Small craft can be launched at the causeway; larger boats on trailers at the dam.

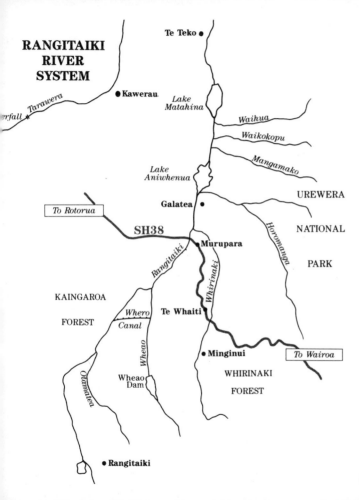

RANGITAIKI RIVER SYSTEM

Te Teko •

• Kawerau

Tarawera

erfall

Lake Matahina

Waihua

Waikokopu

Mangamako

Lake Aniwhenua

Galatea •

UREWERA

To Rotorua

SH38

NATIONAL

Murupara

Rangitaiki

Horomanga

Whirinaki

PARK

KAINGAROA

Whero

Te Whaiti

FOREST

Canal

Wheao

• **Minginui**

To Wairoa

Otamatea

Wheao Dam

WHIRINAKI

FOREST

• **Rangitaiki**

Rangitaiki tributaries

Otamatea Stream

Very clear water, and with overhanging vegetation and timid rainbows, presents quite a challenge. Above the Airstrip Road, dense manuka scrub renders the stream virtually unfishable for 1 km, but the banks are clearer again above this point.

Location Small feeder stream joining the Rangitaiki in the southern area of the Kaiangaroa Forest.

Access Permit required from the Forestry Corporation. Anglers intending to fish in the Kaiangaroa Forest are strongly advised to obtain a map of the area as it is easy to get lost on the network of roads in the pine plantations. Eastern Boundary Road provides river access.

Whaeo River

This river, once world renowned as a fly stream, has been ruined by a hydro-electric power scheme. Rainbows can be taken below the power station, but the river is not recommended. The pools have vanished, water flow has increased and the dense vegetation along the banks makes fishing very difficult.

Whaeo Canal

This connects the Rangitaiki River to the Whaeo hydro-electric power scheme. Contains good stocks of brown and rainbow up to 3 kg. There is a good evening rise in favourable conditions. Try Twilight Beauty or Royal Wulff, dry flies.

Whirinaki River

Beautiful clear river holding a good population of brown and rainbow trout. The most productive water is between Murupara and Te Whaiti. At Murupara, the banks are lined with willows and although fish tend to be small, stocks are high. An imitation willow grub is very effective. Upstream through the gorge there is superb water for nymph or dry fly as fish can be spotted with polaroids. Rainbows predominate and fish up to 2 kg are quite common. Useful nymphs are the Half Back, Hair and Copper and Pheasant Tail; useful dry flies are Dad's Favourite, Coch-y-bondhu and Palmer varieties in sizes 10–14. The upper reaches above Minginui tend to get poached by forestry workers.

Location   Rises in the bush-clad hills of the Whirinaki State Forest, flows by Minginui, Te Whaiti and joins the Rangitaiki north of Murupara.

Access   *Upper reaches*   From S.H.38 just east of Te Whaiti, turn right into Minginui Road. Check with the Forestry Corporation at Minginui before entering the Whirinaki Forest. No permit is required but precautions need to be taken during the fire season. There is a camping ground and cabins are available to rent from the Department of Conservation.

Middle reaches   A logging road follows the true left bank downsteam off S.H.38 just west of Te Whaiti. Access is also possible from Troutbeck and Whirinaki Roads near Murupara. Troutbeck Road runs from S.H.38 opposite Golf Road.

Lower reaches   From Murupara.

Season   1 October — 30 June.

Horomanga River

The lower reaches are shingle and rather unstable but still hold small rainbows which can be tempted with dry fly or nymph. A long walk into the bush is worthwhile as good-sized fish are present in stable pools. This is a spawning stream for Lake Aniwhenua and the fishing can be very good at the end of the season in June or at the opening in October. Run fish respond to a well-sunk nymph or a Taupo-style lure fished deeply through the pools.

Location Rises in the western bush-clad hills of the Urewera National Park and joins the Rangitaiki River just above Lake Aniwhenua.

Access From Galatea.

Season 1 October — 30 June. Fly fishing only is permitted in this river.

Waihua, Mangamako and Waikohopu Streams

Contain good-condition rainbow up to 2 kg. There is gorse and blackberry along the banks in places and some gorgey water to negotiate. The upper reaches enter native bush. They are 'boots and shorts' streams but offer interesting nymph fishing.

Location These three small streams drain the Ikawhenua Range near the Waiohau School, and empty into the Rangitaiki River between the Aniwhenua and Matahina dams.

Access From the Galatea–Te Teko road.

Tarawera River

The river at Kawerau is best fished with a spinner. In the forestry further upstream, there is excellent rough, heavy water containing rainbows averaging 1.5 kg. These can be fished with a weighted nymph, lure on a sinking line or a spinner. In the calmer water, try a Twilight Beauty or a March Brown towards evening.

Location   The river drains Lake Tarawera and emerges from the Tarawera Forest at Kawerau.

Access   At Kawerau. A permit must be obtained from the Forestry Officer at the Tasman Pulp and Paper Mill before entering the Tarawera Forest. Good roads provide easy river access and one can drive to Lake Tarawera.

Although this river is not part of the Rangitaiki system, it is convenient to describe the river below the falls in this section. The Outlet above the falls is dealt with in the Rotorua chapter in the section on Lake Tarawera. Below the pulp and paper mills at Kawerau, the river is polluted and unfishable.

A 4.5 kg rainbow trophy from the Rangitikei River.

70

Urewera National Park

Urewera is the largest national park in the North Island covering almost 200 000 hectares. Ninety percent is forest clad.

There are blocks of privately owned land within the Park boundaries.

The Park has two main valleys, the Whakatane and the Waimana, running from south to north, and two beautiful lakes, Waikaremoana and Waikareiti, lying within its boundaries. Altitude ranges from 150 to 1300 m, and rainfall exceeds 2540 mm. Snow can fall in winter. There are well-cut tracks round both lakes and into some of the valleys, but anglers visiting the Park for the first time are strongly advised to visit the Park Headquarters at Aniwaniwa where maps and information are readily available.

Licence and season   Rotorua licence. Unless otherwise stated, 1 October — 30 June.

Lake Waikaremoana

This lake, which is surrounded by bush-clad hills, lies at an altitude of 580 m above sea level. There are three main inlet streams — the Hopuruahine, Mokau, and Aniwaniwa. The outlet is near Onepoto at the eastern end of the lake where the Waikare-Whenua River has been piped and dammed for hydro-electricity generation. The lake is 220 m deep, and although the weather can be unpredictable in this mountain terrain, there are many inlets offering shelter to boats in adverse conditions. Snowfalls are not uncommon in winter. A well-cut track follows the perimeter of the lake except where it climbs over Panekiri Bluff, and Park Board huts in many of the arms provide overnight accommodation for trampers. It is necessary to carry cooking equipment and fuel, as cutting down native trees for fires is not permitted.

Trout were first liberated in 1896 and smelt in 1948 as a food source. Both brown and rainbow trout are present in the lake and can be caught by all legal

71

methods — harling a fly or trolling a spinner from a boat or spinning and fly fishing from the shore. Favoured spinners are Toby (especially black and red), Cobra and Flatfish. Bully and smelt flies such as Hamill's Killer, Lord's Killer, Muddler Minnow, Killwell No. 1, Mrs Simpson, Rabbit and Red Setter are effective

---

Location   In the centre of the Urewera National Park.

Access   S.H.38 from Rotorua and Murupara to Wairoa, skirts the northern and eastern shores.

Season   1 October — 31 July. For streams flowing into the lake, 1 December — 30 June. Above the Hopuruahine Falls, 1 October — 31 May. Fly fishing only is permitted within 300 m of stream mouths and in the streams entering the lake.

Boat-launching facilities   At Mokau, although the access road is steep, and at Waikaremoana. The road from Murupara is metalled and often corrugated and is unsuitable for towing large caravans and large boats.

Camping   There is a camping ground with cabins at Waikaremoana. Camping is also permitted at Hopuruahine, Mokau and Aniwaniwa.

---

flies. Fish can be stalked along the shore and tempted by a small bully-type wet lure or a dragonfly nymph. There is often a good evening rise in summer and Twilight Beauty and Coch-y-bondhu are hard to beat. Stream mouths are favoured spots for blind lure fishing. In April, May and June a strong run of spawning fish enters the Hopuruahine River and great sport can be had by fishing Taupo-style downstream lure or upstream weighted nymph. Adverse weather can be expected at that time of the year, however. In summer, the same stream is worth exploring with a dry fly or small nymph as is the Aniwaniwa Stream above the falls.

There are still a few very large eels in this lake.

Lake Waikareiti

The lake is not easy to fish as the shoreline is surrounded by bush, making casting difficult. The Wairoa Anglers' Club have a small boat available to

---

Location and access   Can only be reached by walking uphill for an hour on an excellent scenic bush track which begins 200 m from Park Headquarters at Aniwaniwa.

Season   1 October — 30 June.

members. White Bull Bay and Sandy Bay at the top end of the lake offer limited shoreline fishing. Methods as for Waikaremoana. Fish generally are in excellent condition with reddish pink flesh.

Rob and Tim on the Upper Waiau River, Urewera National Park.

Waiau River and tributaries

The river holds a large population of rainbow trout, and fish up to 4 or 5 kg are not uncommon especially near Te Waiotukapiti. The Whangatawhia Stream at Skip's, the Moerangi and Mangakahika streams at Roger's, and the Wairoa Stream at Parahaki all offer excellent back country water.

Location   Drains the bush-clad ranges west and south of Waikaremoana. Flows in a south-easterly direction to enter the sea at Wairoa. The lower reaches are often silt-laden and unattractive. (See East Coat, Gisborne, Wairoa section.)

Access   This river system is for experienced trampers and anglers only. Access is possible from the Okahu Stream at Ngaputahi on S.H.38; a 2-hour tramp to Skip's (Whangatawhia) Hut; and a further 2 hours to Roger's (Te Wairoa) Hut; or from the Mimiha Stream and White's Clearing 8 km west of Ruatahuna; a 5-hour tramp to the Parahaki Hut at the junction of the Wairoa and Parahaki streams. This leads downstream to Central Waiau (1½ hours) and Te Waiotukapiti huts (4 hours); or from Lake Waikaremoana (Maranui Arm), a hard tramp over the Pukekohu Range (9 hours) to Te Waiotukapiti.

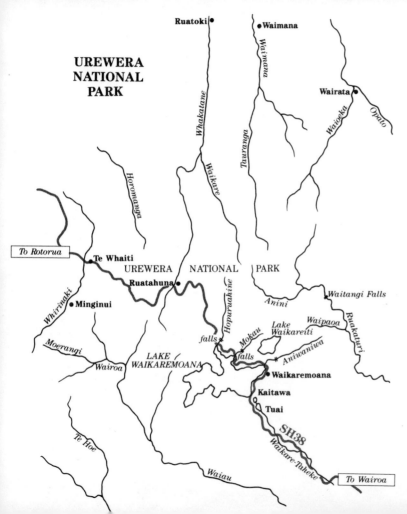

Te Hoe River

This river was ravaged by severe floods in 1981 and again in 1985 and has yet to recover. The river bed has been choked with shingle and logs.

> **Location** Flows parallel to, but south of, the Waiau and outside the Park boundary. Joins the Mohaka River.
>
> **Access** A 4-hour tramp south from Roger's Hut. The headwaters can also be reached via the Kaiangaroa Forest. The lower reaches lie inland from Putorino in northern Hawke's Bay. (See Hawke's Bay District.)

Whakatane River

The best fishing can be obtained well upstream from Ruatoki, as below this point the river is wide and shingly with unstable banks. Both brown and rainbow can be caught in the lower reaches, however, but the water is more suitable for spinning. There is good fly fishing in the upper reaches with fish up to 3 kg present in clear mountain water. A weighted nymph on a long trace is the most effective method.

The Waikare River joins the Whakatane at Waikare

Junction. There is good fly fishing in this tributary, but access is restricted higher upstream as the river traverses private Maori land at Maungapohatu.

Te Rehuwai Safaris operate with horses and guides in this area from Ruatahuna.

Location   This relatively large river rises in the vicinity of Ruatahuna and flows north through the Urewera Park and out through the Bay Of Plenty to the sea at Whakatane.

Access   *Upper reaches*   From Matatua Road just east of Ruatahuna off S.H.38. Tramping is required on a well-marked track from the road end. It descends steeply into the river.
Middle reaches   From the Whakatane River track either from the Ruatahuna end as described or from the Ruatoki end in the Bay Of Plenty.
Lower reaches   From Whakatane, Taneatua or Ruatoki.

Season   Below the Owaka Stream confluence, 1 October — 30 September. Above this, 1 October — 30 June.

Some years ago while tramping the Whakatane Valley with family and friends, I fished **a likely looking**

run below the Waikare Hut. My quiet fly-fishing efforts were suddenly interrupted by a genial Maori on horseback, threadlining off the back of his horse. He splashed from pool to pool and when a fish was hooked he merely wound it up and stuffed it into a saddle-bag without even bothering to dismount.

Waimana River

Fishing can be patchy but promising areas are just above the township, below Olgivie's Bridge and in the region of the Lions' Club hut. The river is usually very clear in the upper reaches and offers sport to all types of legitimate fishing. Rainbow predominate.

A small feeder stream, the Raroa, also offers fly water at Waimana township. Below Waimana, an

---

Location   Drains the Kairaka and Kahikatea ranges and flows north, parallel to, but east of, the Whakatane River. Flows out through the Bay Of Plenty at Waimana and joins the Whakatane at Taneatua.

Access   Road access from Waimana township 30 km from Whakatane.

Season   Below Reid Road Bridge, 1 October — 30 September. Above the bridge, 1 October — 30 June.

---

evening rise in the more sedate willow-lined stretches can excite the purist. Wading is generally safe. In the lower reaches early in the season, trout chase whitebait, elvers and smelt. A smelt fly fished across and down on a medium sinking line can be most effective. There are some very deep pools in these lower reaches and a popular swimming hole close to S.H.2 is over 6 m deep.

Waiotahe River

This river east of the Waimana is not recommended. I have yet to see a fish in the upper reaches, although there are a few small rainbow in the lower reaches.

Waioeka River

This river has had a chequered history. It drains very steep country, and has been prone to massive flooding in the past, seriously depleting fish stocks. However, deep permanent pools can be seen from the road and these provide reasonable fly and spin water. The upper reaches in the bush contain some good-sized rainbow,

if one is prepared to walk. A small tributary at Opotiki, the Otara River, holds reasonable stocks of small rainbow. Upstream of the Waioeka-Opato confluence, fly fishing only is permitted.

Location   Although this river lies north of the Park boundary, it is convenient to deal with it in this section. Flows north from the bush-clad hills east of the Waimana and Waiotahe valleys to join the Opato River at Wairata in the Waioeka Gorge on S.H.2, then follows S.H.2 to the sea at Opotiki.

Access   From the Waioeka Gorge road. The upper reaches over the bridge above Wairata flow through private land and permission should first be obtained from the landowner.

The Horomanga River rises from the eastern Ureweras but is dealt with in the Rangitaiki section. Similarly the Ruakaturi is described in the Gisborne — Wairoa section.

East Coast, Gisborne and Wairoa

These three areas lie in the Rotorua Acclimatisation Society's district. There are three main river systems supporting a significant trout population — the Motu, the Waiapu and the Wairoa river systems. Many of the East Coast rivers were severely turned over by a collossal flood in 1981, and again by Cyclone Bola in 1988. Some streams in this area become too warm in summer, while others are affected by farm run-off and clear felling on the banks and become silt-laden rapidly in a fresh. The only rivers that offer really good fishing are the inaccessible Motu, the Ruakaturi, Hangaroa and the Waiau. The Waioeka and the greater part of the Waiau are described in the Urewera section and only the lower reaches of the latter are considered in this chapter. The area can be fished with either a Rotorua or a New Zealand licence. Unless otherwise stated, the season opens on 1 October and closes on 30 June.

Wairoa River system

This extensive waterway empties into the sea at Wairoa. The major tributaries of this river which drain the eastern Urewera National Park are the Waiau, Waikare–Taheke, Ruakituri and Hangaroa rivers. The Wairoa River is formed at Te Reinga Falls north of Wairoa township by the confluence of the Ruakaturi and Hangaroa rivers. The Wairoa River itself is large, rather sluggish and unattractive, best suited to spin fishing. It contains both brown and rainbow trout with the latter predominating. Access is from Frasertown on S.H.36, the 'back' road to Gisborne via Tirinoto. There is an open season on this river from 1 October to 30 September.

Waiau River

The lower reaches of this river are rather unattractive and the water easily becomes heavily silt-laden in a fresh. However, there is good fishing at Putere, inland from Raupunga on S.H.2. Follow Waireka Road from Putere Lakes to Otoi. There are pools and runs containing mainly rainbow, and fish up to 3 kg can be anticipated. All methods of fly fishing and spinning will take fish. The Putere Lakes, Rotonuiaha, Rotoroa and Rotongaio also hold trout, but for some reason these are difficult to catch. There is an open season below the Waikare–Taheke confluence and on the Putere Lakes.

Location   Drains the inaccessible bush-clad ranges south of Lake Waikaremoana, flows in a south-easterly direction across farmland, joins the Waikare–Taheke River near the Patunamu Forest, and together these rivers empty into the Wairoa at Frasertown.

Lakes Kaitawa and Whakamarino (Tuai)

These small lakes near the outlet of Waikaremoana hold large brown trout and fish up to 9 kg have been taken. Although these lakes have a limited shoreline, fish can be taken on a Hamill's Killer, Red Setter or Mrs Simpson fished on a slow sinking line especially at dusk. The lakes are reserved for fly fishing only.

Other small lakes in this area hold trout. The largest are Lakes Wherowhero and Kiriopuhae.

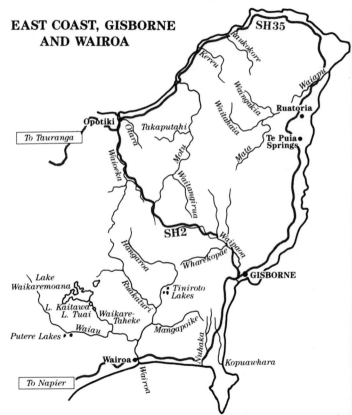

EAST COAST, GISBORNE AND WAIROA

Waikare — Taheke River

Fast-flowing river overgrown in places and not easy to fish. Contains rainbow averaging 1–1.5 kg and is best fished with spinning gear or downstream lure.

> **Location**   Drains Lake Waikaremoana but has been dammed for power generation near the outlet, forming lakes Kaitawa and Whakamarino (Tuai).
>
> **Access**   S.H.38 from Waikaremoana to Frasertown follows this river downstream.
>
> **Season**   Open season 1 October — 30 September downstream from the Piripaua power station.

Mangapoike River

Supports a small population of rainbow trout, but no liberations have been made in recent years as the water quality is marginal in summer.

> **Location**   Drains in a south-westerly direction to join the Wairoa River at Opoiti north of Frasertown.
>
> **Access**   From the Mangapoike Valley road, which leaves S.H.38 just south of Frasertown.

Ruakituri River

This relatively inaccessible river provides superb nymph fishing. The stretch of water from the Erepeti Bridge to Papuni would be hard to better in New Zealand. The river holds an astounding quantity of trout in excellent condition, although with increased angling pressure from tourists arriving by helicopter, there is a danger that the fishing will fall off. Trout are not good to eat from these waters as they often have a muddy flavour, so catch-and-release methods are strongly recommended. The river holds brown and rainbow in equal proportions and fish average 2 kg with an occasional fish up to 7 kg, especially above Waitangi Falls.

Care is needed when wading, but the river can be crossed quite readily at the tail of most pools. Beware of slippery rocks! Fish are often difficult to spot as there are some very deep runs and pools. In high summer with low water conditions, fish can be seen and stalked with a dry fly or nymph.

This is unstable papa country and the great disadvantage of this river is its propensity to become rapidly silt-laden in a fresh. It may take two or three days to clear. Any weighted nymph in sizes 12-16 will take fish but caddis imitations seem most appropriate due to the high density of this insect on the stream bed. There is often a vigorous evening rise and fish will accept a Twilight Beauty. However, at times a nymph can be more effective during the rise than a dry fly.

There is a large area of fishable water and if one is prepared to tramp, the Waipaoa tributary upstream from Papuni and the river above Waitangi Falls offer almost unlimited possibilities. These are strong fish and

---

Location Drains the heavily bush-clad high rainfall country north of Lake Waikaremoana, flows in a south-easterly direction and joins the Hangaroa River at the spectacular Te Reinga Falls.

Access *Upper reaches* From Ruakaturi Valley Road, which leaves S.H.36 at Te Reinga. This provides good road access to the river. Tramping experience is required if a visit above the Waitangi Falls is contemplated or the Waipaoa tributary explored.

Rua's Track crosses the Anini Stream between Waimaha Station and Mangapohatu. Considerable tramping experience is required, but there are rainbow in the Anini tributary. This stream can be reached after a 5-hour tramp from Waimiha Station.

Downstream from the Waitangi Falls to the confluence with the Hangaroa River is reserved for fly fishing only.

I well remember landing four brown trout during a morning's fishing but losing the same number of rainbow. Four kg nylon broke like cotton! A friend who regularly fishes this river has taken to the water and swum down after fish on a number of occasions in order to land his fish.

The slow-flowing stretch above Papuni holds double-figure browns but these are very difficult to deceive.

Campsites are available with no facilities, but permission should first be obtained from local runholders. The manager of Papuni Station also appreciates an approach before crossing land to visit the Waipaoa or the Waitangi Falls.

Hangaroa River

The best water is above Tahunga. This river gets very warm in hot summer conditions except in the upper bush-clad reaches behind Tahora Station. Fish can be spotted and taken on dry fly, nymph, lure and spinner. Rainbow predominate but there are browns as well, and fish average 2 kg, with an occasional one up to 4 kg. In parts, the river is rather sluggish. Fish have been caught by floating a small Half Back nymph on a long trace downstream. In the evening, a Sedge has proved deadly.

> **Location** Rises in the eastern Urewera National Park north of Rua's Track. Flows along the western boundary of Tahora and Waimiha Stations, turns east to Hangaroa and then flows south to Te Reinga where it joins the Ruakituri River.
>
> **Access** The Taumata road, from Rere, leads to Tahunga and Waimiha Station. Permission is required from the station manager. Most water can only be reached through private farmland.

Tiniroto Lakes

There are a number of small lakes at Tiniroto that hold small rainbow. The largest, Rotokaha, is easily visible from S.H.36 just south of Tiniroto. These lakes are best fished from a boat as their shorelines are swampy and rush infested. Open season all year round on these lakes.

Nuhaka River

Supports a small population of rainbow, but because of poor water quality in summer, no liberations have been made recently.

> **Location** Flows in a southerly direction parallel to, but west of, the Kopuawhara River to enter Hawkes Bay at Nuhaka near the Mahia Peninsula.
>
> **Access** Turn off S.H.2 onto the Nuhaka River road 5 km north of Nuhaka.

Kopuawhara River

Although this stream is not self-sustaining, it is regularly stocked as the water quality is good. There is productive and interesting dry fly and nymph fishing for small rainbows.

> **Location** Rises in the Whareata State Forest north of the Mahia Peninsula and flows south to enter the sea at Oraka Beach.
>
> **Access** Travel east from Nuhaka to Opoutama, then north on Mahanga and Kopuawhara Roads. A permit is required from the Forestry Corporation to enter the State Forest.

Wharekopae River

This river silts easily from land erosion, and liberations have ceased as a result. However, the river does support a small population of brown trout.

> **Location**   Rises from the eastern slopes of the Huiarau Range, flows east to Rere and then northeast to join the Waipaoa River near Te Karaka.
>
> **Access**   This is relatively isolated hilly sheep country and the roads are narrow, winding and unsealed. The small settlement of Rere, west of Gisborne, where the Rere Falls complement the scenery, provides the best access.

Motu River and tributaries

This large river system drains some of the most inaccessible country in New Zealand. The river is now protected as a wild and scenic river and is popular for rafting, the most suitable method of transport along some stretches. It is an excellent self-sustaining fishery despite a large eel population.

Motu River

The upper reaches wind through cleared farmland before leaving Motu. The river is prone to flooding, and below the confluence with the heavily silt-laden Mangatane River, the water deteriorates to such an extent that fishing is not worthwhile. Around Matawai and Motu, the river holds a population of small brown trout that can be taken on flies or spinners. An occasional fish up to 2 kg is caught. As with most brown trout, skill is required to achieve success. Fish are not easy to spot in the brownish water. In the inaccessible area not serviced by road there are larger fish as well as some 'grandfather' eels.

> **Location**   Drains the northern Huiarau Range and the rugged Raukumara Range between Gisborne and Opotiki. Flows on a northerly course through heavily bush-clad, precipitous country to enter the sea south of Te Kaha.
>
> **Access**   From Matawai on S.H.2 at the eastern end of the Waioeka Gorge, a road runs north down the true right bank to the settlement of Motu. The Motu Falls road is washed out beyond Waitangirua Station.

Motu tributaries

Only two are worth describing but other inaccessible side streams do contain trout. A deerstalking friend has captured fish on a 'nickel spinner' in the Mangatutara Stream to supplement his diet when hunting.

Waitangirua Stream

This stream is a delight for the dry fly angler and holds brown trout up to 4 kg. It is a 'boots and shorts' stream with clear pools and runs, the reaches upstream from the 'back whare' flowing through native bush. On a recent trip in high summer I stalked and hooked 6 fish on a Royal Wulff, but only one, weighing 3 kg, was in good condition. The others were thin and fought

---

Location and access Permission must be obtained from Waitangirua Station on the Motu Falls road before approaching this stream. Tramping experience is needed as the river is an 8 km walk from the station buildings. A very rough four wheel drive clay track can be negotiated in dry weather only. Access can also be obtained via Whatatutu and Okaihau by following down Jackson Stream through private land.

---

poorly. The stream is well stocked but occasionally heavily poached.

Takaputahi Stream

I first heard of this river some 15 years ago when a skin diver boasted about the large brown trout he had managed to shoot in a hole. There are deep holes in this river but the trout population tends to vary from year to year. However, fish up to 3 kg are not unusual and can be taken on flies and spinners. There is an evening rise, but after dark, try fishing a Hairy Dog deeply through these pools. The river flows through partly cleared farmland and bush on a shingle bed.

Good camping is available at the Whitikau campsite, where the road first meets the river.

Location This river flows in an easterly direction to enter the Motu north-east of Toatoa.

Access Turn off S.H.35, 10 km east of Opotiki on the road to Waiaua and Toatoa. From Toatoa, the Takaputahi road leads to the river. Toatoa can also be reached by travelling on a winding shingle road from Matawai. This is very inaccessible rough country.

My information with regard to spear fishing proved to be correct as on a recent visit with my daughter and a friend we surprised a young Maori lad walking unashamedly along the road carrying snorkel, face mask and spear.

Waiapu River tributaries

The Waiapu tributaries drain the Raukumara Range in the vicinity of Mt Hikurangi, west of Ruatoria. These rivers follow a north-easterly course until the Waiapu itself enters the sea 15 km south of East Cape. The Waiapu and the Mata River downstream from the Waingakia confluence have little in the way of good holding water. A shifting shingle bed and water that is frequently silt-laden is not conducive to good fishing. However, some of the many tributaries rising in more stable country hold fish. A number of these are inaccessible except to adventurous anglers or hunters who enjoy fishing.

The fish population has a rather tenuous hold in this river system so catch-and-release is strongly encouraged. In 1981, colossal flooding severely affected most of these rivers. Releases were made by helicopter in 1985 into the Waitahaia, Mangaokura, Oronui, Waingakia and Raparapaririki streams. The Ruakokore River further north also hopefully gained some benefit from a similar liberation. I have visited only two of these tributaries and although I caught rainbow averaging 1.5 kg the area is not highly recommended.

Waingakia River

Unstable shale and great eroded cliff faces dominate this valley, but the river has stable pools and runs. Rainbow respond well to a sunk nymph, downstream lure and a spinner.

Location and access   Turn off S.H.35 at Aorangi south of Ruatoria, travel inland to the Makaraka School, cross the Mata River and follow the narrow Horehore Road up the true left bank of this river to the road end. The Waingakia seeps out under boulders into the Mata River.

Waitahaia River

Rainbow up to 2 kg can be taken by the adventurous 'boots and shorts' angler who is prepared to walk. The river is interesting to fish, as trout can be spotted in stable pools and runs.

Location and access This is even more inaccessible than the Waingakia, being inland from Te Puia Springs. Turn off from S.H.35 south of Tokomaru Bay and travel inland to Mangatarata, Huiarua and Owhena on the Ihungia road. Access to the river is through private farmland, the river lying in a deep valley.

The Raukokore and Kereu rivers, flowing north and entering the sea between Waihau Bay and Te Kaha, also hold a few rainbow but are not recommended because of their unstable nature.

Hawke's Bay District

This district has a wide variety of fishing water. In the north rivers traverse steep hill country. Across the Heretaunga Plains, the rivers are not unlike the Canterbury rivers — wide, shallow, unstable and shingly. In the south, rivers have cut deep gorges in the soft rock and limestone. The climate also resembles Canterbury's in that dry warm westerlies are the prevailing winds, and during the hot summer months streams with a shingle bed often dry up and flow underground. So fishing is better in the smaller tributaries both early and late in the season.

Note:— The Ripia and Waipunga rivers (See Kaimanawa — Kaweka Forest Park section) can be fished on a Rotorua or Hawke's Bay licence.

Season	Unless otherwise stated, 1 October — 30 April.

Mohaka River

(See Kaweka Forest Park for upper reaches.)
The reaches from Pukaututu to Te Hoe provide extensive stretches of heavy, relatively inaccessible water. Below Te Hoe, the river becomes very large and is more suited to spinning. Travel is often difficult due to gorges and bluffs and the river is not easy to ford in many places. Despite these limiting factors, there is excellent brown and rainbow fishing for fly and spinner and fish up to 3 kg are not uncommon. An angling companion recently watched a fish of about 6–7 kg from the top of a cliff. Fish can be spotted, and a weighted Hare and Copper or Half Back nymph on a long trace can be very effective. There is an evening rise although one would need to be camped by the river to take advantage of this. When spinning, use a heavy spinner in order to get sufficient depth in the larger pools. This river is highly regarded by local anglers and holds a large stock of good-sized trout.

Location   *Middle reaches*   Flows from Pakaututu in a north-easterly direction to enter the sea south of Wairoa at Mohaka.

Access
● From Pakaututu north of Puketitiri;
● S.H.5, the Taupo–Napier road, crosses the river 45 km north of Napier. McVicar's Road runs for a short distance up the true left bank. The Waitere road follows downstream on the true right bank.
● The Pohokura road, from Tutira north of Napier, leads to the river opposite the Te Hoe junction;
● The Willow Flat road leaves S.H.2 near Kotemaori;
● S.H.2 crosses near its mouth at Raupunga.

Season   Downstream from the Pakaututu Bridge there is an open season 1 October — 30 September. Upstream from the bridge, 1 October — 30 April. Above the Mangatainoka River junction, a Rotorua licence is needed.

HAWKE'S BAY DISTRICT

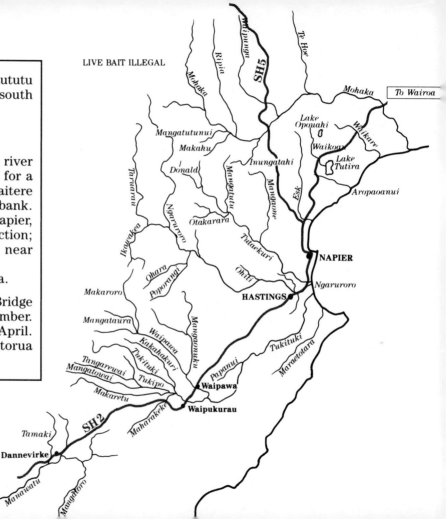

Shona Fokerd fly fishing the Upper Mohaka River.

Inungatahi Stream

Severely damaged by floods in 1981 and 1985. Has not recovered yet. Small fly stream sometimes containing good fish and at other times is barren. Flows through rather unstable steep country and discolours easily after rain. I have visited this stream on two occasions. On the first visit, I took 3 good fish; a rainbow on a Coch-y-bondhu and two browns on a Pheasant Tail nymph, all weighing around 2 kg. On the second visit, I did not see a fish.

Location   Rises near Puketitiri, follows a north-easterly course and empties into the Mohaka just upstream from the main road bridge (S.H.5).

Access   Through private farmland off McVicar's Road.

Te Hoe River

Recently ravaged by floods, the bed has been turned over and blocked with log jams. Before this, the river offered good back country rock and stone type fishing, but it will take some time to recover.

Location   Upper reaches have been referred to in the Urewera National Park section. Drains the bush-clad ranges south of the Waiau River to join the Mohaka at Te Hoe.

Access   Very difficult as the junction is in isolated country. Turn off S.H.2 at the Tutira store on the Pohokura road, which is narrow and winding. The road brings you to the Te Hoe–Mohaka junction. The Mohaka must be crossed to reach the Te Hoe and this is not always easy.

Lake Tutira

Some years ago, this lake was severely affected by eutrophication. With Government assistance, the local farmers, Catchment Board, Acclimatisation Society, Forest and Bird Society and the County Council, aided by scientific research, have restored the water quality. It is now crystal clear and only polluted by swans. The lake is willow fringed on its western shore and fishing is best carried out from a boat either harling a fly or casting along the fringes of the natural weed beds. Fish up to 2 kg can be caught but their condition is not very good.

Location   38 km north of Napier on S.H.2.

Access   S.H.2 follows the western shore.

Season   The lake is overstocked with rainbow so there is no bag limit and there is open season from 1 October to 30 September.

Boat-launching facilities   No motors are permitted on this lake. Although there is no boat ramp, there are good launching facilities from the camping and rest area at the southern end of the lake.

Lake Opouaki

Small attractive lake 2 ha in area. Best fished from a dinghy although difficult to launch. No motors are permitted. The lake contains fontinalis (brook trout), up to 1 kg, and some residual rainbow. Lead lines are permitted and harling a red-bodied Mrs Simpson or a spoon on such a line offers the best chance of success.

Location   Turn left at the Tutira store on the Pohokura road.

Waikare River

Unfortunately, this river was badly affected by floods in 1981 and 1985. It has still not recovered. The river flows through deep gorges and is more suited to the boots-and-shorts style of fishing. Before the floods, there were limited stocks of small rainbow and brown trout.

Location   At Putorino, north of Lake Tutira.

Access   Crossed by S.H.2. The Matahoura road gives access to the headwaters while the Glenbrook road, off the Waikare Coast road, gives access to the lower reaches.

Waikoau and Aropaoanui Rivers

The Waikoau is a tributary of the Arapaoanui River.

Contains a small population of brown and rainbow trout from 0.5 to 1.5 kg. The rivers have a rocky, stable bed and flow through attractive gorge country. Catch-and-release would benefit these streams.

Location   Just south of Lake Tutira.

Access
● S.H.2 crosses the Aropaoanui River just north of the Devil's Elbow.
● Aropaoanui Road leaves S.H.2 at the summit of Devil's Elbow and follows down the true right bank of the Aropaoanui River;
● Waikoau Road leaves S.H.2 just before the Tutira store and crosses the Waikoau Stream.

Esk River

Severely affected by floods over the years, the last in 1983. There are large sea-run browns in the lower reaches although this area is rather unattractive to fish. They will take a sunk nymph or a smelt fly.

The upper reaches flow through typical Hawke's Bay sheep country and contain both brown and rainbow up to 2 kg, although stocks are not high. An hour's walk upstream from the end of the Ellis–Wallace road is worthwhile for the energetic angler. Size 14 Pheasant Tail, Hare and Copper and Hare's Ear nymphs are recommended.

Location   Rises in the Maungaharuru Range and flows in a southerly direction to meet S.H.5 near Eskdale 15 km north of Napier.

Access
- *Lower reaches*   From S.H.5.
- *Upper reaches*   From the Ellis–Wallace road, which branches off S.H.5 just west of Eskdale. Travel on this road for 12 km to a delightful picnic spot.

Tutaekuri River and tributaries

Tutaekuri River

Wide unstable shingly river holding mainly rainbow averaging 1 kg. In October and November fish feed on smelt, elvers and whitebait in the lower and middle reaches. Schools of trout tend to follow this food source upriver so fish may not remain in the same pool from one day to the next. Use a smelt fly on a slow-sinking or even a floating line and fish across and downstream. In the hot summer months, weed becomes a problem in the lower reaches. There is often a good evening rise, especially in the upper reaches, and nymphs and spinners take their share of fish.

Location   Headwaters drain the Kaweka Ranges, flows east across the Heretaunga Plains through the outskirts of Taradale, then to the sea just south of Napier.

Access
- *Upper reaches*   Flag Range Road, off the Napier–Taihape road.
- *Middle reaches*   From the Puketapu–Dartmoor road.
- *Lower reaches*   From Taradale. S.H.2 crosses at its mouth.

Season
- Above the Mangatutu River, 1 October — 31 May.
- Below the Mangaone River, 1 October — 30 September (excluding May, which is the duck shooting season).
- Between the Mangatutu and Mangaone rivers, 1 October — 31 April.

Mangaone River

Restricted to fly fishing only. Flows through a deep gorge in the upper reaches with good pools holding mainly rainbow. Fish average 1 kg, but the odd fish up to 3 kg can be expected. There is good fishing at the junction with the Tutaekuri. The usual nymphs and small lures take fish. The Hawke's Bay Acclimatisation Society recommend Wickham's Fancy and Red Tipped Governor early in the season and Blue Dun later.

Location   Drains the Te Waka Range, flows in a southerly direction and joins the Tutaekuri at Dartmoor west of Napier.

Access
- *Upper reaches*   Through private farmland off Glengarry Road which leaves S.H.5.
- *Middle reaches*   From Rissington.
- *Lower reaches*   From Dartmoor.

Mangatutu River

Small stream fished best early in the season but not generally recommended.

Location and access   Off Waldon Road after passing through Dartmoor and Waihau Roads.

Ngaruroro River and tributaries

Ngaruroro River
(See Kaimanawa Forest Park for upper reaches.)

Beware of the westerlies which bring rain to the Kawekas and discolour the river. The same fishing methods apply to this river as for the Tutaekuri. Smelt fly fishing can be good in October — November in the middle and lower reaches; in the summer, weed becomes a problem. Favoured spots include the Ohara and Otamauri stream mouths at Whanawhana and the Ohiti stream mouth past Fernhill.

The Ohiti itself carries trout but it is difficult to fish because of overhanging willows. There are some deep, reasonably stable pools in the Ngaruroro where the river runs hard against a bank, and the fishing is improved where vegetation overhangs the river. Nymphs, dry flies, lures and spinners can all be used in these situations. Rainbow averaging 1 kg with an occasional larger fish can be expected. For the spin fisherman, try a black and gold Toby or a gold spoon.

Location After leaving the Ruahine Ranges, this large shingle river flows east across the Heretaunga Plains to share a mouth with the Tutaekuri River.

Access
- *Upper reaches* From the Napier–Taihape road at Kuripapango.
- *Middle reaches* Through Fernhill on the Ohiti road to Whanawhana.
- *Lower reaches* From the Fernhill Bridge where a good track runs down the true left bank for some distance. The Pakowhai road crosses lower down.

Season
- Above the Taururau, 1 October — 31 May.
- Between the Chesterhope and Fernhill bridges, the river can be fished all year.
- Downstream from the Taururau (except between the above bridges) to the sea, the river can be fished all year except during May.

Ohara River

Fishes best early in the season before water flows are reduced. Holds rainbow averaging 1 kg and the usual methods will take fish. The middle and upper reaches run in a deep gorge and access is difficult.

Location Source in the Ruahines, then flows north-east, joins the Poporangi and enters the Ngaruroro opposite Whanawhana.

Access
- Turn off S.H.2 at Longlands; take the Maraekakaho road then the Kereru road and then Big Hill Road.
- Matapiro–Whanawhana road takes you near the confluence of the Ohara and Ngaruroro rivers. The braided Ngaruroro can be crossed if care is taken.

Season 1 October — 30 May.

Taruarau River (See Kaimanawa Forest Park.)

Tutaekuri–Waimate Stream

'Deep ditch' difficult to fish but contains a good population of rainbow in cold, clear spring water. Water-cress and weed add to the difficulties. Fish average 1 kg, but the stream contains larger fish. Night fishing and the evening rise are the most productive times. Try a night fly or a fly spoon on a high density line. During the rise a Twilight Beauty or a Coch-y-bondhu should bring results.

Location Rises from springs near Swamp Road and enters the Ngaruroro upstream from the Chesterhope Bridge.

Access From the Pakowhai road, by walking over the stopbank opposite the Pakowhai Store; from Chesterhope Road which crosses the stream and through private land.

Twin Lakes (Diamond Lakes)

No boats are allowed. The lakes hold many Loch Leven trout which will rise to a dry fly or take a cobra.

Location Near Kuripapango on the Napier–Taihape road.

Access From Castle Rocks Road. From the carpark walk for 45 minutes to the first lake.

Tukituki River and tributaries

Tukituki River

This is the most popular river in Hawke's Bay. The upper reaches above Waipukurau are best fished early in the season as the shallow runs become too warm in summer. The lower reaches below the Waimarama Bridge fish well in October — November when trout are chasing whitebait, smelt and elvers. In the hot weather, weed becomes a problem. The river has a

Location Rises in the Ruahine Ranges, flows south-east to Waipukurau and then turns north-east to enter the sea at Haumoana near Hastings.

Access Very well serviced by roads on both banks. The Middle Road follows the true left bank from south of Hastings to Patangata. The lower reaches flow just east of Havelock North.

Season Open 1 October — 30 September where it passes through the Tukituki wildlife refuge and between the junction of the Tukipo River and the Mount Herbert Road extension. From 1 October — 30 September excluding May, downstream to the sea from S.H.50 road bridge, near Ashcott. Elsewhere, 1 October — 30 April.

wide shingle bed except around Patangata where there are areas of papa. The stones are very slippery for wading and care should be taken. Brown and rainbow trout are present in good numbers although the latter predominate.

A Blue Dun fishes well during the mayfly hatch and in the upper reaches, a Stone fly is most effective. The most popular area lies between the Patangata and Tamumu bridges.

Waipawa River

Shingly willow-lined river which fishes reasonably well all season. Contains mainly rainbow averaging 0.5–1 kg, and is best suited to fly fishing. The Mangaonuku and Tukituki junctions are favoured spots. Try nymphs and dry flies during the evening and small wet flies (Red Tipped Governor) during the day.

Location Drains the Ruahines and flows on a south-easterly course to join the Tukituki near Waipawa.

Access
● *Upper reaches* Springhill, Makaroro and Caldwell Roads.
● *Middle reaches* Stockade Road off Ongaonga Road.
● *Lower reaches* S.H.2 crosses in the Waipawa township.

Season Within the Waipawa boundaries, 1 October — 30 September. From S.H.50 bridge to the Tukituki junction, 1 October — 30 September (excluding May, the duck shooting season).

A 3 kg sea-run brown from Tukituki.

Mangaonuku River

Artificial fly only in this river.

Best fishing can be obtained early in the season from the junction upstream to the limeworks. Contains mainly rainbow averaging 1 kg, but the occasional fish of 3 kg is caught. Being spring fed, the river rarely discolours. Try Coch-y-bondhu, Molefly, Greenwell's Glory and Black Spider dry flies; Pheasant Tail, Half Back, Hare's Ear and Hare and Copper nymphs; Red Tipped Governor, March Brown and Hardy's Favourite wet flies; and Hamill's Killer, Mrs Simpson, Parson's Glory and Smelt pattern lures in the small sizes.

> **Location**   Flows in a southerly direction from its spring-fed source near Poporangi to join the Waipawa.
>
> **Access**   Waipawa–Tikokino road, Brow Bridge on the Tikokino road, and Stockade Road from Ruataniwha, which gives access to the Waipawa junction.

Makaroro River

Fishes best early and late in the season. Shingly bed is reasonably stable in the lower reaches but gorgey and more inaccessible in the upper reaches. Mainly rainbow around the 1–1.5 kg mark.

> **Location and access**   Lies 46 km from Waipawa on the Ongaonga and Makaroro roads. At the T junction of the Makaroro and Waharara roads, drive down a track to the Waipawa–Makaroro confluence.

Tukipo River

Fly fishing only.

Lower reaches early and late in the season. Typical shingly willow-lined tributary. Flies as for the Mangaonuku. Junction with the Tukituki is a favoured spot.

> **Location and access**
> ● *Upper reaches*   From S.H.50 between Ashcott and Takapau.
> ● *Middle reaches*   From Balfour Road off S.H.50.
> ● *Lower reaches*   Through private farms off the Ashcott–Waipukurau road.

Maharakeke River

Fly fishing only.

This river is suffering badly from weed growth thought to be due to freezing works effluent. Contains both brown and rainbow trout, but is very difficult to fish at the present.

> **Location and access**   Spring-fed tributary of the Tukipo which joins this river just west of Waipukurau. Crossed by S.H.2. The Hatuma Limeworks road follows up the true right bank.

The Makaretu and Mangatewai rivers also contain fish but are not recommended.

Maraetotara River

Fly fishing only.

This is a beautiful spring-fed stream which has unfortunately deteriorated over the past few seasons. It is thought to be due to clearing vegetation from the banks in the upper reaches, thereby silting the spawning beds. Above the bridge, the river is still overgrown in parts and this provides food and cover for fish and offers the angler a real challenge. In many places a small flick cast is all that can be achieved. The fish are very wary and lie in crystal-clear rock pools.

The best chance of success lies in deceiving trout with a carefully presented size 14 nymph or a small dry fly at dusk. There are fish present above and below the falls and many anglers have watched the large fish cruising in the falls pool safe from even the most adventurous angler. Only brown trout are present and fish up to 2.5 kg are not uncommon.

There is good fly fishing below the bridge across private farmland.

> **Location**   Rises on Mt Kahurunaki, flows for 18 km in a northerly direction east of Havelock North and reaches the sea at Te Awanga.
>
> **Access**
> ● *Upper reaches*   Through private property off the Maraetotara Valley road.
> ● *Middle reaches*   Off the Maraetotara Valley road. The Havelock North–Waimarama road crosses the river.
> ● *Lower reaches*   Private access off the road to Ocean Beach.

Manawatu River

The upper reaches are in the Hawke's Bay District and these are dealt with in the Wairarapa area.

Upper Waikato River and Hydro Lakes

There are five lakes in this area — Maraetai, Whakamaru, Atiamuri, Ohakuri and Aratiatia. All have been formed from damming the Waikato River. In addition, a number of streams draining into these lakes or into the river itself hold fish and are worth investigating. A Rotorua licence is required to fish this area. There is an open season on all the lakes from 1 October to 30 September, but the season for the streams is from 1 October to 30 June. Unfortunately, eutrophication is a problem on all lakes and weed and algae growth, expecially during the warmer summer months, makes fishing difficult.

The most productive time to fish is either early in the season or during the winter months. A boat is a decided advantage. Browns and rainbows up to 3 kg are present although the average weight of fish caught is considerably less than this. At Queen's Birthday Weekend each year, the 'Big Three' competition is held. Prizes are awarded to angler/hunters skilled and lucky enough to bag a deer, a wild pig and a trout over the weekend.

Lake Maraetai

Formed in 1952. With high summer water temperatures, blue-green algae present a problem and fishing is inconsistent. During the winter, try trolling a Tokoroa Chicken, Toby and Cobra spinners. If possible, avoid weed beds. Fish average 1 kg and both brown and rainbow trout in reasonable condition can be caught.

The Mangakino Stream holds fish but is overgrown and difficult to fish.

Location At Mangakino on S.H.30.

Access From Mangakino, where there is a boat-launching ramp.

Lake Whakamaru

This hydro lake was created in 1956. There are large areas of shallow water, and weed is a problem. Fly

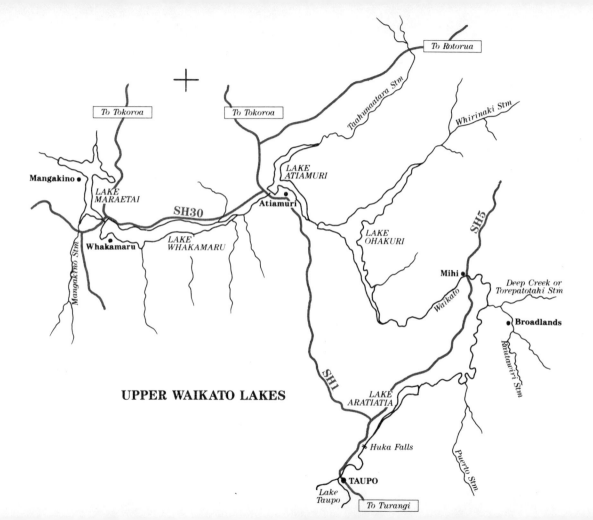

UPPER WAIKATO LAKES

fishing at stream mouths after dark can be rewarding with Hairy Dog, Black Phantom or Maribou lures on a slow-sinking line. Boat fishing as for Lake Maraetai. Holds brown and rainbow in good condition averaging 1.5 kg.

Location   Upstream from Mangakino township. S.H.30 crosses the dam.

Access   Boat-launching facilities at Whakamaru hydro village. S.H.30 follows the northern shore.

Lake Atiamuri

This small, deep lake was formed in 1958. The fishing methods are similar to those described above. Fish average 1 kg.

Location   S.H.1 between Taupo and Tokoroa crosses the Waikato River just below the Atiamuri Dam.

Access   Boat-launching facilities at Atiamuri.

The Taahunaatara Stream draining into this lake is worth investigating and can be reached off S.H.30 between Atiamuri and Rotorua. There is good dry fly fishing during the beetle hatch in November and December, especially above the road bridge on S.H.30. Three streams join in this region — the Pokaitu, Matahana and Rahopakapaka.

Lake Ohakuri

This large lake was formed in 1961, and is popular for water sports in summer. Has the same weed problem, and fishing methods are the same as already described. Holds both brown and rainbow in reasonable condition, averaging 1 kg.

The Whirinaki Stream draining into this lake holds rainbow. Flows through farmland and can be reached via Ngakuru off S.H.30 between Atiamuri and Rotorua from Mangatete or Whirinaki Valley roads. The lower reaches can be fished from a boat but not during summer because of algae and weed.

Location   Turn off S.H.1 just south of Atiamuri. The road through the forest is well signposted.

Access   There is a boat ramp and picnic area at the end of this road.

Lake Aratiatia

Not as popular as the other lakes described in this section. Similar fishing methods apply. Trout average 1.5 kg but are generally in poor condition. Restocking has not taken place since 1971.

Location and access   From Wairaki Village off S.H.5.

Upper Waikato River

The river is deep, quietly flowing and subject to flow variations. These are controlled by the flood gates at Taupo and anglers need to be wary. The river is often low at 9 am but rises at 10 am. A variety of fishing methods are used but spinning and downstream lures are favoured. Small stream mouths are top locations and nymph fishing can be successful at these spots. The mouth of Puerto Stream can be reached from Vaile Road, off Broadlands Road; the Waiehu and Kaiwhitiwhiti mouth across farmland just south of Broadlands Forest, and Deep Creek or Torepatutahi Stream from a road running north-east from Broadlands township. Try a Red Setter or Hamill's Killer, or a weighted Hare and Copper nymph. At dusk,

there is often a good sedge rise and a sedge imitation skimmed across the current can be most effective.

Location   The most popular stretch is between the Aratiatia Dam and the head of Lake Ohakuri. The section between Lake Taupo and the Huka Falls 13 km downstream also holds fish but access is limited.

Access   Ohaki Road off S.H.5; turn off north of Wairaki Village; or from side roads off Broadlands Road, running north from Taupo along the true right bank; also from River Road off S.H.1 just north of Taupo.

The Puerto Stream off Broadlands Road, the Rautawiri Stream off Earles Road and the Kaiwhitiwhiti Stream off East Road all contain rainbow and are worth investigating. Access is generally across private dairy farms. Weed can be troublesome in the hot summer months, so visit these spring-fed streams early in the season. Dry fly and nymph fishing in very clear water where fish can readily be spotted makes for challenging fishing. On two visits to these streams I have taken 6 fish on a size 14 weighted nymph. The largest was 1.5 kg in fair condition. However, I scared off twice that number!

Taupo District

Ova from European brown trout (*Salmo trutta*) were brought to the South Island from Tasmania in 1867 and to Taupo in 1886. Rainbow trout (*Salmo gairdnerii*) ova from Sonoma Creek in San Francisco Bay were obtained in 1883, hatched in a pond in the Auckland Domain and liberated in Lake Taupo in 1897. All the rainbow trout in New Zealand have originated from this one shipment. Food sources in this lake were plentiful and included the striped kopuku (a small native greyling), koura (freshwater crayfish), inanga (whitebait) and cockabully. Trout thrived and by 1910 fish weighing 9 kg were being caught. In the 1920s the food supply was depleted to such a low level that fish lost condition and the Government introduced netting to reduce stocks. Then in 1934, a smelt (*retropinna*) was introduced as a food source. This was very successful and now constitutes the main food supply for Taupo trout.

Between April and September, sixty percent of trout in Lake Taupo run up rivers entering the lake to spawn. Spent fish (kelts or slabs) return to the lake at much the same time that smelt school into the shallows and river mouths to spawn, i.e., October — December. Fish feed voraciously to regain condition. Fry that have hatched and survived enter the lake 9 to 12 months later as fingerlings 15-20 cm long. In 2 to 4 years, these fingerlings reach maturity, and so the cycle continues.

Lake Taupo

The lake, the largest in New Zealand, is 40 km long, 30 km wide and covers more than 600 sq km. It has an average depth of 120 m, the deepest point being 160 m, and lies 360 m above sea level.

This fishery fully deserves its worldwide reputation, as it offers a wide variety of superb angling water. Over 1200 tonnes of trout are landed each year. The average weight of each fish caught is approximately 1.6 kg. Fish over 4 kg are not uncommon although most of these are brown trout. A friend recently witnessed an overseas visitor nonchalantly walking up the Tokaanu Wharf carrying a rainbow weighing 6.8 kg, landed while trolling.

The movement of trout in the lake follows the smelt life cycle. From October to January 'smelt fishing' can be had along the shoreline and at river mouths. From October to the end of May feeding fish can be caught at river mouths, but shoreline fishing is unproductive after January. From the end of May, when river water temperatures equal lake temperatures, fish feed in the deeper waters of the lake and only enter stream mouths briefly before running up to spawn. Deep trolling then becomes an effective method.

Fish can still be caught during the winter months, but action tends to be slower in the lake, whereas river fishing comes into its own.

Fly fishing at river mouths (This information also applies to stream mouths on lakes other than Lake Taupo).

Trout feed along the lip where the river delta drops off into deeper water and along the edges of the current where it merges with the lake water. It is important to stand back a few metres from the lip as fish often take the fly during the retrieve as it passes over the lip. Wading is usually necessary, however, and waders are essential to protect against the cold water. In shallow mouths, thigh waders are adequate but chest waders are needed for deeper water. False casting in the air is recommended at shallow mouths as excessive water disturbance, even at night, frightens feeding fish. Most Taupo stream mouths can be fished with either a medium sinking or floating line. A weight forward line will enable a longer cast to be made, an important factor when fishing pressure is high. Generally, a strong on-shore wind makes fishing difficult, but when the current parallels the shore, the prime spot may be 50 m along the beach. A light on-shore breeze may be conducive to good fishing.

A few seasons ago, my friend and I were camped in the lupins at a stream mouth in the western bays. It was mid-February, a good time to catch brownies. For three successive nights a strong on-shore easterly wind drove surf onto the beach creating unfishable conditions. A couple of anglers came, tried a few casts into the wind and departed. Then, as if by magic, the wind dropped about 9.30 p.m. each evening, the lake calmed and the rip straightened up. By 11 p.m., my friend and I had our limits; every cast was a take. We had never had such exciting steam mouth fishing.

There is no substitute for experience as each stream mouth has its own characteristics. However, when the fishing is slow a number of options may be tried. Try changing position, but before doing so always ask other

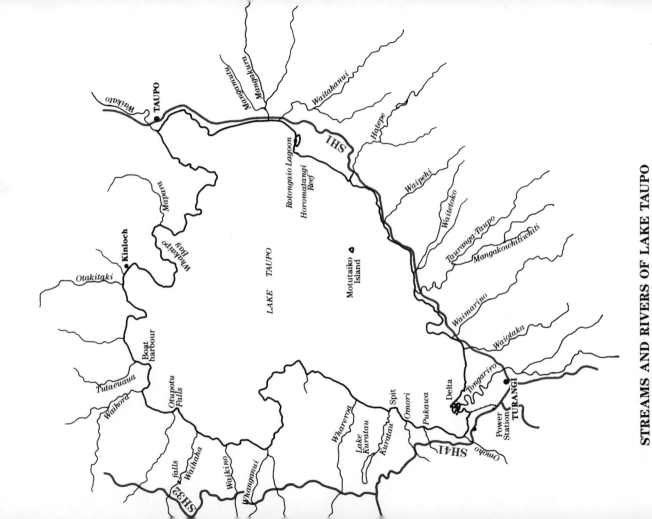

STREAMS AND RIVERS OF LAKE TAUPO

anglers and do not force your way into the prime spot unless there is an obvious gap or you are joining the end of the line. Sometimes fish do not feed along the lip and it may be worth wading well out and casting into the tail of the current. Do not fish in front of another angler and if in doubt, check before making such a move. Other tactics when the fishing is slow include changing lines, trying a smaller fly or changing fly patterns. Some flies do not swim well and even changing flies of a similar pattern can make a difference. Altering the speed of the retrieve may also bring success. Remember, your fly should swim to resemble a smelt or, if fishing slowly and deeply, a koura.

At very small stream mouths, fishing improves if the current runs straight out into the lake. A shovel and two polythene bags filled with shingle can prove very useful, but do not leave the bags for others to trip over. Periodically resting such water for 15 minutes can also entice trout back to the shallows but it may be difficult to convince others to cooperate with this action. Fishing is generally better on dark, moonless nights, but do not be discouraged by other conditions as I well remember taking a limit on a Red Setter when the moon was full and bright.

During the day, when fish are smelting through the rip, action can be fast and furious or totally frustrating. Trout can be seen gorging on smelt and although many of these fish will be kelts, fishing is invariably fascinating. Try a very small smelt fly, even as small as a number 10 or 12. When all else fails a nymph fished along the edge of the current can bring surprising results.

Flies   *At night:*   Maribou flies, Hairy Dog, Fuzzy Wuzzy, Black Phantom, Scotch Poacher, Guardsman, Black Rabbit or Craig's Night-time in sizes 2-6. I prefer the larger sizes but a stronger trace is advised up to 5.5 kg. When all else fails at night, try a daytime smelt pattern or a luminous bodied fly.
During the day: Green Smelt, Taupo Tiger, Split Partridge, Grey Ghost, Mallard Smelt, Hawk and Silver, Parson's Glory, Jack's Sprat, Doll flies or Ginger Mick in overcast conditions. Sizes 6-10 preferred. I watched a friend take a limit on a Hairy Dog one bright sunny day.

Smelt fishing along the beaches

Walking the beaches looking for smelting fish on a hot bright day is my favourite Taupo fishing. November and December are the prime months. Shorts, sandshoes, polaroids, hat and sunscreen are essential. Schools of fish can be seen at times breaking the surface and throwing caution to the winds in their efforts to feed on these tiny spawning fish. A quick cast and a fast retrieve are required using a floating line and a small smelt fly. In very calm conditions, casting at fish frightens them. A sinking line casts no shadow and if the fly is landed well away from cruising fish and retrieved as the trout approaches, a take can be anticipated. This is an exciting way to fish.

Fishing the rivers

Trout run up Taupo rivers from March to November. The heaviest runs occur after a storm and heavy rain. By July, the rivers are full of fish and by September many fish will be spent and drifting back to the lake. Trout tend to lie in the deeper parts of pools under banks where there is maximum cover. Each pool has a favoured lie, some have more than one, but to be successful, an angler must ensure that the lure or nymph being fished reaches a depth sufficient to entice a take. This means 'dredging' the bottom.

Downstream lure: In the smaller rivers, a light 2.5 m rod and a medium sinking line are all that is required. In the Tongariro, a 3 m rod and a high density line is advisable. A trace of 2 to 2.5 m is sufficient, as a longer trace tends to allow the fly to float higher. Use a trace of 3.5 to 5 kg breaking strain in the larger rivers, lighter in the smaller streams. The lure should be cast across the river or even slightly upstream in a big pool, allowed to sink deeply as it drifts with the current, swung through the lie and retrieved.

The 'take' usually occurs at the end of the swing. There is nothing so exciting as a fresh run of rainbow of 2.5 kg smashing the fly. Mending the line to take up the slack is advised as the line begins to swing. Subtle variations can be made by altering the speed of the retrieve.

Favoured lures include Rabbit flies, Red Setter, Hairy Dog, Mrs Simpson, Dappled Dog, smelt varieties, Mallard patterns, and Leslie's Lure. Many new patterns are being produced, some with fluorescent bodies, but it is difficult to improve on the first two listed.

Upstream nymph

With the introduction of lightweight rod materials, the same sized rods can be used for both methods of fishing. A weight forward Nos. 8-10 floating line should be used for the Tongariro, while a lighter Nos. 6-8 can be used on the smaller streams. Naturally, the line weight should match the rod.

For the smaller streams, one weighted nymph is sufficient, but in the heavier water many anglers use two heavily weighted nymphs placed from 12-60 cm apart. The short trace attached to the distal nymph is tied to the bend of the hook of the proximal nymph. When fishing heavy water, use a long trace up to 5 m in length, but casting can become very difficult with this rig especially in a strong wind. Pulling up your parka hood may not be primarily to protect you from the weather!

A long cast upstream ensures your nymph has plenty of time to sink and drift through the lie, scraping the stones on the bottom. Allow the nymph to float down naturally with the current and not drag. Most anglers use an indicator or float attached to the end of the line, which could be a quill, a bunch of wool or a piece of polystyrene. When the indicator deviates in its downstream course, stops or sinks, an immediate strike must be made before the fish rejects the deception. Some anglers now run their trace through a Fuller's Earth and glycerine mix to reduce surface tension on the nylon, allowing it to sink rapidly.

All water can be explored with a nymph and it is surprising how fish may choose to lie in pockets of very rough water. A wide range of nymphs will take fish although the smaller sizes are more consistently accepted. For this reason, the proximal nymph is often large (long shank size 8) and heavily weighted while the distal nymph can be size 12–14 and still be fished deeply.

Favoured nymphs and deceptions include Hare and Copper, Bug Eye varieties, Half Back, White Caddis, Pheasant Tail, Muppet and Glow Bug.

Favoured locations

Trout can be caught anywhere in Lake Taupo. Stream mouths are top locations but many rocky points around the lake can also provide good fishing. Trout tend to cruise the 'blue line', the junction between inshore shallows and deeper water. Before selecting a spot to fish, make certain there is not a strong on-shore wind.

Stream and river mouths
Eastern lake shore

Mangakura Stream

Enters the lake 1 km north of the Waitahanui mouth. Can be worth exploring during the smelting season and at night. You are unlikely to be disturbed by other anglers.

Waitahanui

The most famous river mouth on Lake Taupo, not because of the number of fish caught but because of the 'picket fence' or line of anglers easily viewed from the main highway. This is not the place for a beginner as a long cast with a weight forward medium sinking line is essential if one is to compete with other anglers. After a westerly storm, the current will be forced along the beach and 200 m or so can be fished without wading. The mouth is well known as a place to catch large brown trout, usually during the nights of February and March. Smelt flies are effective during the day and the usual night patterns after dark.

Otupatu Creek
Drains the Rotongaio Lagoon. Good smelt fishing along the beach south of the outlet at the foot of the white cliffs. Worth trying at night.

Hatepe River mouth
When other rivers are dirty, have a look at the Hatepe. You can drive to the river mouth.

Waipehi Stream
There is a delightful rest area beneath kowhai trees at this stream mouth. It is very shallow and rocky. A floating line is essential and there is better fishing after dark. Fishes well most of the year, even in winter.

Waitetoko Stream
Comments as for Waipehi Stream (above). Very small stream entering the lake at Manowharangi Bay.

Tauranga-Taupo River mouth
This mouth is dangerous for wading and is generally fished from an anchored boat. The boat is positioned to enable the angler to cast a fly on a heavy sinking line over the very deep lip, pause for a moment and then begin a slow retrieve. Fishing can be excellent at times, generally at night.

Southern lake shore
All these streams have easy access. However, as with any new spot it pays to view the area during daylight before fishing after dark.

Waimarino River mouth
Can only be fished when the lake is low as a long wade is needed in order to fish over the 'blue line'. At this point the current is barely perceptible and change of position may be necessary before the right spot is found. Use a medium sinking line, cast into deep water and slowly retrieve. A landing net is essential, otherwise fish will need to be beached some 100 m behind you.

Fishes well all year but beware of a strong north-easter. Be confident and carry a length of cord to string fish together on your belt; it may save a long walk when the action is all on.

Waiotaka mouth
Walk south along the beach from the yacht club and carpark. Shallow mouth best fished after dark, has a reputation for brown trout.

Tongariro mouth or the Delta
The Delta is a prime fishing spot but can only be reached by boat. Wading along the soft pumice lip is hazardous as the water is 20 m deep. Selecting one of the mouths to fish is governed by the wind direction.

The boat should be anchored with the transome barely hanging over the lip. Use a high density line and a similar technique to that used at the Tauranga–Taupo mouth, except the water is deeper and a longer interval is advised before beginning the retrieve. The line can be pointing directly beneath the boat. During the day, use a smelt fly and after dark the usual night pattern. In the winter, when trout are entering the river to spawn, fish can even be taken on a Glow Bug or Muppet. However, this seems little short of snapper fishing. In favourable conditions, the fishing at the Delta can be quite superb.

Tokaanu tailrace

From November to February when smelt are running, the screens at the Tokaanu Powerhouse impede their upstream progress. Schools of these tiny fish gather in confusion and are easy prey to marauding trout. Good fly fishing can be obtained from the banks of the tailrace especially upstream from the main road bridge although the quality of the surroundings may not equal the quality of the fishing. However, the tailrace has a reputation for large fish. Fish can also be taken from the Tokaanu wharf and from the mouth of the tailrace close by.

Tokaanu Stream, Slip (Omoho) Creek, Omori and Pukawa streams

All can be reached from S.H.41 between Tokaanu and Kuratau. They should be fished at night with a floating line and smallish night flies. False air casting is strongly recommended and there is room for only 2 or 3 rods. Can be fished all year round with success. It is illegal to fish these streams except at their mouth.

Kuratau River mouth

This is a very shallow wide delta and is safe to wade. Excellent fishing can be had when fish are smelting. Use a floating line during the day and after dark. The Kuratau Spit a few hundred metres south of the mouth is well worth fishing as the 'blue line' runs close inshore.

Whareroa River mouth

Can be reached by car from the Kuratau Hydro road. Use a similar technique as for all shallow river mouths. When the current runs parallel to the shore, browns can be caught at night 50 m south of the actual mouth. In the smelting season, there is good river mouth and beach fishing.

Western lake shore

Access is generally by boat.

Whanganui Stream mouth

This is the most inaccessible of the western bays and generally access is by boat. It is almost 20 km from either Kuratau or Kinloch. Road access through Wharerawa Block is unreliable and at times hazardous because of washouts in the pumice road. Over the past few years, the river mouth has become too shallow for sheltering a boat. There is very good stream mouth and beach fishing during the smelting season. A medium sinking or floating line is recommended. If the action is slow at the rip try at the southern end of the beach close to the bush.

Waikino Stream mouth

Gushes out of a rocky cleft between Whanganui and Waihaha bays. There is a peg to tie a boat to on the north side. A heavy sinking line is needed to reach fish clearly visible deep beneath the current. Occasionally, night fishing can be excellent at this spot even off the rocky shelf on the southern side.

Waihaha River mouth

Access is by boat; the nearest boat ramp is Kinloch. The bay can also be reached by walking down a steep track from the end of Waihaha Road, off S.H.32. Although the mouth changes during storms, it usually remains sufficiently deep to shelter a boat. Fishing is best when the current flows in the direction of Whakatonga (Richwhite) Point. When fish are smelting, exciting fishing can be had from the point itself, especially if a mate sits high on the hill and spots. Beach fishing for smelting fish is good in November and December. A diving friend told of empty cans and bottles sunk off the end of the rip — discarded refuse from boats anchored upstream in the river. I have had more than one confrontation with such boaties.

Two or three km upstream are the Tieke Falls. They can be reached by boat and the falls pool offers good fishing.

Otupoto Falls

Enter the lake at the southern end of Waihora Bay. Fly casting from a boat can be done although the usual method of fishing is trolling.

Waihora River mouth

Access is by boat from Kinloch. There is good sheltered anchorage close by in Boat Harbour at Kawakawa Point. Excellent night fishing can be had at this mouth and fish smelt along the beach in November and December. A few seasons ago I was lucky enough to spot, hook and land a 3.5 kg maiden hen off this beach on a Hawk and Silver. Large brown trout often lie deep in the lower reaches of this river but are very wary.

Chinaman's Creek (Tutaeuaua Creek)
Enters the southern end of Kawakawa Bay. Can be reached by a 15-minute walk from the end of Puketapu Road, a branch road off Whangamata Road. Usual methods apply to this shallow mouth. Only holds two rods comfortably.

Northern lake shore

Otakitaki Stream
Can only be reached when the lake is low by wading round a rocky point at the western end of Whangamata Bay.

Whangamata Stream
Reached by walking west along the beach from Kinloch.

Mapara Stream
Enters the eastern end of Whakaipo Bay. This mouth is very popular and heavily fished. A strong southerly or westerly wind will make it unfishable. Floating or sink tip line, false air casting and the usual night flies should bring reward providing there are not too many rods present. Then the angler with the longest cast has the best chance of success.

Rivers flowing into Lake Taupo

Waitahanui River
Because it is spring-fed this river has a consistent flow and seldom discolours. The river bed is fine pumice and the banks are stable. As the water is deep and quite swift, nymphing is difficult and the deeply sunk lure accounts for nearly all the fish taken. Successful anglers use a high density line and a slow retrieve. Many bury their rod tip in the river to ensure the fly swims through the lies.

The best fishing can be had in March through to September. After a good southerly storm, scores of fish enter the river. These can easily be seen from the main road bridge. This river is not for the faint-hearted, and because of the intense angling pressure, fishing ethics have largely disappeared. Above the bridge there are 7 km of good water and anglers find less pressure in these upper reaches.

A wide variety of flies are used, including Parson's Glory, Red Setter, Rabbit variations and smelt patterns. I have found a size 4-6 Orange Rabbit with a long tail to be a good teaser but a friend swears by a Green Smelt. The crucial factors are probably not the fly but the depth and the way it swims through the lie.

Hatepe or Hinemaiaia River

Note　The river is closed above the main road bridge from 31 May to 1 December. Fishing is not permitted within 300 m of the lower dam. There is a sign at this point.

Above the bridge　There is superb nymph water although casting can be tricky in places due to overhanging vegetation. Hooked fish also have a chance to escape by tangling round snags. Use a trace measuring roughly 4 m and false air cast. In shallow lies, endeavour to land the nymph well above sighted fish, with the line behind. In the deeper pools, fish are not so easily frightened and lining the fish may not be detrimental. Many nymph patterns will take fish, but the smaller sizes are more effective. Try Pheasant Tail, Hare and Copper, White Caddis, and Half Back patterns all weighted in sizes 12-14.

Below the bridge　The water is more suited to sunk downstream lure methods. Lures can also be very effective above the bridge especially after a fresh run.

Try Rabbit flies, smelt patterns, Red Setter and Parson's Glory in sizes 6-8 on a medium sinking line.

Tauranga–Taupo River

Note　Above the Rangers' Pool where the Mangakowhitiwhiti Stream enters, the river is closed from 31 May to 1 December.

This delightful river is recommended for novices as wading is safe and casting is generally unimpeded by vegetation.

Fish run from April to September and as is the case with all Taupo rivers, the most productive time to fish is after a storm and heavy rain. During fine weather and low water conditions, the fishing can be hard.

I remember a day in August when heavy rain began at midday, breaking a long dry spell. By evening, the river had risen to cover the car park at the end of the quarry road. The river was unfishable but trout were running up the edge of the muddy torrent in great numbers even in the grass. Next morning the river level had dropped and the fishing was superb. I took five fat silver fish on a Red Setter.

The river can be fished after dark but few anglers take advantage of this fact. Weighted nymphs and Glow Bugs also take their share of fish. In the deeper pools such as the Rangers', Windmill and Cliff, lies tend to be towards the tail of the pool. When lure fishing, cast well across the pool with a sinking line and wait 20 seconds before commencing the retrieve. In this way, the lure should swim deeply through the lie. Pools can also be fished with one or two well-weighted nymphs on a 4.5-5 m trace and a floating line. Darker fish that are spawning should be returned and only fresh-run fish kept.

Use the same flies and nymphs as for the Hatepe with the addition of Bug Eye, Muppet, Glow Bug, Dappled Dog, Jock Miller, Mrs Simpson and the usual night flies.

After 1 December, good dry fly and nymph fishing can be obtained on mending fish, especially in runs above the Rangers' Pool. The upper gorge provides a challenge for the adventurous angler although access off Kiko Road can be a problem unless a motorbike is used.

Access   Drive through Winstone's Quarry up the true right bank from the main road bridge. There are good tracks on both sides of the river.

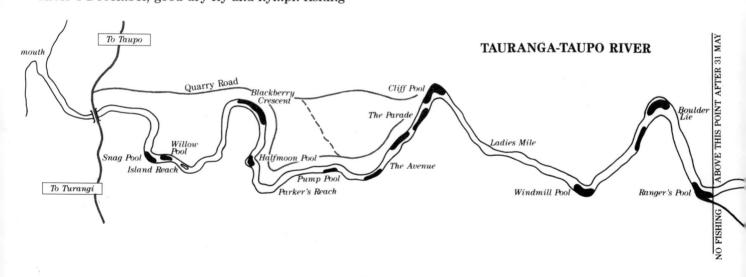

TAURANGA-TAUPO RIVER

mouth

To Taupo

Quarry Road

Blackberry Crescent

Cliff Pool

The Parade

Boulder Lie

Willow Pool

Ladies Mile

Snag Pool

Halfmoon Pool

Island Reach

The Avenue

Pump Pool

To Turangi

Parker's Reach

Windmill Pool

Ranger's Pool

ABOVE THIS POINT AFTER 31 MAY

NO FISHING

Waimarino River

Note   Closed season above Korohe Crossing from 31 May to 1 December.

Small river which fishes much better after a fresh and when there is a good volume of water in the river. Below S.H.1, the river is overgrown with willows. Up to the Korohe Crossing the same applies and in my experience, fish pass rapidly through these reaches to the pools and runs above Korohe Pa. Here there is excellent water but fish are wary and need to be approached cautiously. The usual lures and nymphs are effective, but as the river is small and clear use the smaller sizes.

Access
- *Lower reaches*   From S.H.1. Just south of Motuoapa.
- *Middle and upper reaches*   From Korohe Road.

Waiotaka Stream

Smaller but similar stream to the upper Waimarino and fishing methods are the same. The lower reaches are not recommended but the stretch running through the prison is ideal nymphing water.

Access   By courtesy of the Department of Justice. Arrangements can be made through the Superintendent of Hautu Prison.

Tongariro River

Many excellent books have been written about this world-famous river, describing the pools in considerable detail. Despite reduced water flows taken for power generation, the river still deserves its reputation.

Below the main road bridge, the river is shingly and willowed. Above the bridge, the scenery improves with clumps of manuka and native bush softening the river. Nymph fishing predominates in the upper river, while lure fishing is more popular in the Major Jones and Lonely pools and below the bridge. Both methods can be effective in all parts of the river, but lure fishing tends to be hard during fine weather and reduced water flows.

The river can be crossed at certain spots but great care should be taken as the rocks can be slippery with algae and the current swift. Pools can change significantly during floods and lies that were productive before the flood may become barren and silt up. This has occurred to some extent recently in the Whitikau and Island pools, whereas the Lonely Pool has improved. Try the Hydro Pool on the true right bank near the mouth of the Mangamawhitiwhiti Stream for large brownies. You will need to be on the river early to obtain this favourite spot.

Greig's Sports Shop in Turangi has published a detailed guide for the Tongariro River. The angling pressure on some of the pools is intense but do not be discouraged when your favourite stretch of river is fully occupied as most pools and runs hold fish, especially after a fresh. Seek out some of the unlikely spots and you could be pleasantly surprised.

In the warm summer months, good dry fly fishing can be enjoyed on mending fish and there is little angling pressure at this time of the year. Try an imitation sedge and skim it across the surface of the pool.

Etiquette To avoid unpleasant confrontations which can ruin a day's fishing, always ask another angler fishing the pool where you can start fishing. It may be obvious if others are nymphing; you can join the queue downstream. Similarly, if others are all downstream lure fishing, start at the top of the pool. However, problems arise when an angler is fishing a Glow Bug downstream on a sinking line.

Season Above the Whitikau Stream, 1 December — 31 May. Elsewhere, 1 July — 30 June.

Access Generally good as the river is well tracked by the Department of Conservation. Above the main road bridge, S.H.1 follows the true left bank from Turangi to the Poutu River. At this bridge, there is a shingle road giving access to the upper pools — Breakaway, Fan, Boulder, Blue, Sand and Whitikau. There is vehicle access off S.H.1 to the Red Hut Pool and the Birch Pools (through the hatchery), and off Taupehi Road to the Hydro, Breakfast, Major Jones, Island and Judges Pool. The Lonely and Bridge pools lie either side of the main road bridge. Below the bridge, Grace Road follows the true right bank downstream from S.H.1 giving access to the Stones (off Herekiekie Street), Bain, Log, Reed, Jones, the Parade, Smallman's Reach, DeLatours, and Graces. Access to the true left bank below the main road bridge can be obtained from Turangi township.

Begg's Pool below the hydro dam can be approached from the Desert Road on the Kaimanawa Forest Park road. This is a launching place for rafting, and anglers fishing the Whitikau, Sand and Blue pools are often disturbed by rafts.

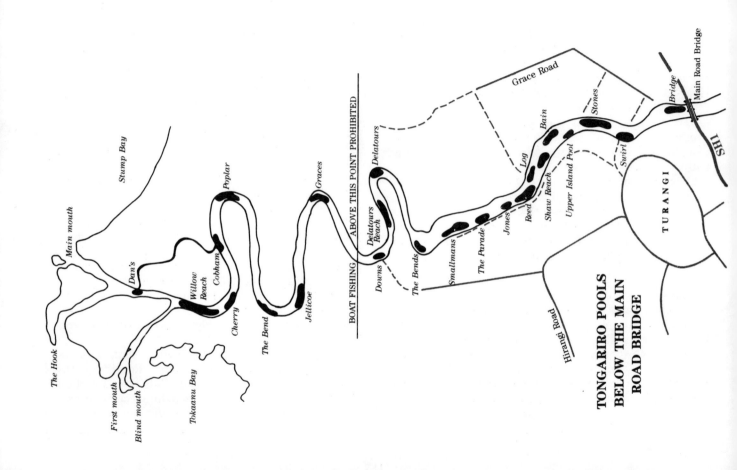

TONGARIRO POOLS BELOW THE MAIN ROAD BRIDGE

The Hook

First mouth

Blind mouth

Tokaanu Bay

Main mouth

Stump Bay

Dan's

Willow Reach

Cobham

Poplar

Cherry

The Bend

Jellicoe

Graces

BOAT FISHING ABOVE THIS POINT PROHIBITED

Downs

Delatours Reach

Delatours

The Bends

Smallmans

The Parade

Jones

Reed

Log

Shaw Reach

Bain

Upper Island Pool

Stones

Swirl

Grace Road

Bridge

Main Road Bridge

SH1

TURANGI

Hirangi Road

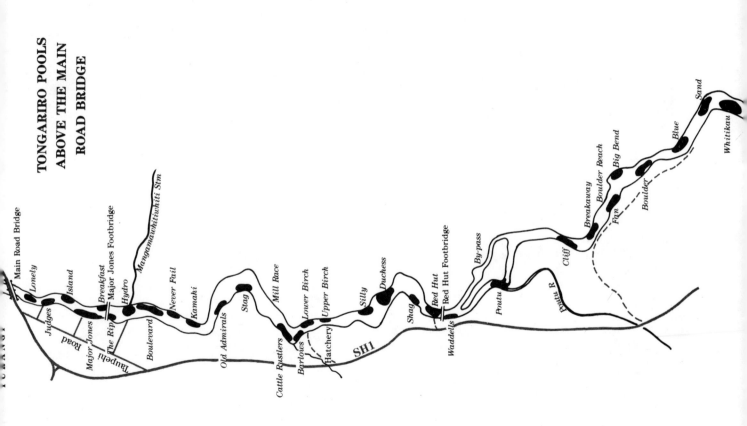

TONGARIRO POOLS ABOVE THE MAIN ROAD BRIDGE

Main Road Bridge
Lonely
Judges
Island
Major Jones
Taupehi Road
The Rip
Breakfast
Major Jones Footbridge
Hydro
Boulevard
Mangamawhitiwhiti Stm
Never Fail
Kamahi
Old Admirals
Stag
Mill Race
Cattle Rustlers
Barlous
Lower Birch
Upper Birch
Hatchery
SH1
Silly
Duchess
Shag
Red Hut
Red Hut Footbridge
Waddells
By-pass
Poutu
Poutu R
Cliff
Breakaway
Fan
Boulder
Boulder Reach
Big Bend
Blue
Boulder
Whitikau
Sand

117

Boulder Pool, Tongariro.

Trolling and harling

More fish are taken in Taupo from a boat than by any other method. Remember, it is illegal to troll or harl within 300 m of any stream or river mouth. The only exceptions are the Waikino and Otupoto Falls.

Launching facilities   Small boats can be launched from most beaches. There are boat ramps for larger boats at Taupo on the Waikato River outlet, at Acacia Bay, Kinloch, Kuratau Spit, Waihi, Tokaanu Wharf, Motuoapa and at Four Mile Bay or Wharewaka.

Safety advice   Maori sometimes called the lake Taupo-hau-rau — 'Lake of a hundred winds' — because of the strong southerly winds that can spring unexpectedly. A short, steep 1.5 m chop can prove troublesome even for a 5 m boat and a 60 hp outboard. Anglers are advised to carry the same safety equipment as if fishing offshore at sea.

Harling a fly   When fish are smelting, from September to February harling a smelt fly on a fly rod and a high density line can be most effective. Boat speed must be kept to a minimum either by using a small auxiliary outboard motor or slowing down the boat by towing a sea anchor. Let out the whole length of fly line and 20 m of backing to ensure the fly sinks sufficiently. The trace should be 5-6 m long.
  Favoured flies include Parson's Glory, Ginger Mick, Orange, Yellow and Green Rabbit, Taupo Tiger, Grey Ghost and other smelt varieties, Hamill's Killer, Green and Yellow Orbit in sizes 6-4.

Trolling a spinner   In the autumn and winter, trout become bottom feeders and trolling a spinner on a wire or lead line along the drop-off or 'blue line' brings results. The wire line will sink deeper than the lead line but is more difficult to handle and tangles readily. Do not turn the boat too sharply when using either of these lines. When a fish is caught, turn the boat and troll over the same area. If using a monofilament line, it pays to let out 80–100 m. The breaking strain should be 8–9 kg. Some anglers attach a length of lead line to the monofilament. With a lead line, experiment using different lengths in order to find the optimum depth. The number of colours can be used as a measurement and guide once optimum depth has been found.
  Favoured spinners include Toby, Cobra, Flatfish and Zed Spinners of varying colours and sizes.

Favoured trolling locations   Trout can be caught anywhere in the lake, even in the middle, but good areas include Whanganui Bay, Kawakawa Bay, Whangamata Bay, the Whakaipo Reef, Mine Bay, Rangatira Point, off the Waitahanui mouth, and the Horomatangi Reef located off Rotongaio.

Spinning in Taupo   Spinning is only permitted in the lake. No spinning is permitted in any of the streams flowing into Lake Taupo nor within 300 m of any stream mouth.

Few anglers use this method in Taupo, but for a young angler learning to fish spinning is easier to start with than a fly. All three varieties of reel (closed and open-faced spinning reel and baitcasting reel) can be used. Apart from the spinner no added weights need be employed. During the smelting season, a small bright silvery spinner can be most effective.

Poutu River

This river is open all season but it is not easy to fish. There is a short stretch of water upstream from the main road bridge and below the falls that is worth exploring. Access from a track following upstream from the main road bridge along the true left bank.

Lake Rotoaira

Boat fishing — either harling a fly, trolling a spinner or fly casting from a drifting boat — is necessary as the shoreline is swampy and difficult. Only rainbow are present and stocks are high with fish averaging 1–2 kg. Fly casting is probably the most productive method and flies used include Hamill's Killer, Killwell varieties,

Rabbit flies and Red Setter. Use a medium sinking line. Best fished from February to May. The size and abundance of fish has been reduced by the alteration in lake water flow as a result of hydro development.

Licence   Taupo, plus a special licence from the Maori owners of the lake. The lake is privately owned. There is an open season.

Location   S.H.47 circles the southern shores while the Te Ponanga Saddle road from Turangi and S.H.41 skirt the northern shore.

Access   Boat-launching facilities at the Rotoaira Fishing Camp and for small boats at the foot of Te Ponanga Saddle near the tailrace and at the Wairehu Canal.

Lake Otamangakau

The headwaters of the Wanganui River were diverted to form this lake in 1971, as part of the Tongariro power scheme. The lake is surrounded by flat tussock country and the view of the mountains in the Tongariro National Park certainly adds to its scenic qualities.

The lake covers an area of 150 ha and holds some magnificent trout. Rainbows predominate and fish up to 6 kg have been taken. Trout food in the lake is plentiful and consists of dragonfly larvae, mayflies, caddis, snails and midge larvae. There are no smelt or bullies in this lake. All legal methods can be used but the majority of fish are caught from boats either harling a lure or fly casting a lure, nymph or dry fly. Traditional lure fishing from the shore with either a slow or fast sinking line is effective as is nymph fishing with a floater. Trolling a spinner or spin fishing from the shore is difficult because of the weed banks. The lake is subject to wide fluctuations in water level, and conditions can change rapidly.

Try a Hamill's Killer, an Orange Rabbit or a large black fly at night, especially near the Wairehu Canal outlet. With the floater, use a very slow retrieve and a Dragon Fly or Half Back nymph. Even an imitation cicada can be deadly. In the evening, fish will rise to a Twilight Beauty or Royal Wulff. Be prepared for

large, superbly conditioned fish that strip 50 to 70 m of line off your reel and then bury themselves deep in a weed bed. You are doing well if you hook 3 or 4 fish in a day and only land one of them.

Kuratau Dam

Difficult to fish from the shore because of swamp and weed. Fish can be taken off the dam using a sinking line and a lure. Fish average 0.9 kg. Angling pressure is low.

Location and access   Off S.H.32, on the Kuratau Hydro road.

Waihaha River

Location and access   S.H.32 crosses the river well above the Tieke Falls. Downstream from the bridge, there is nymph water holding small rainbows. Be cautious crossing the stream as there are some deep slots in the rocky bed.

Location and access   On the opposite side of the Te Ponanga Saddle road to Lake Rotoaira (S.H.47). Two access roads are signposted Wanganui Intake, Te Whaiau Dam, Otamangakau Dam, Boat Ramp, and Wairehu Control Gate.

Season   1 October — 31 May.

Kaimanawa and Kaweka Forest Parks

Location The Kaimanawa Forest Park lies east of Lake Taupo and the Desert Road (S.H.1). The Park covers more than 85 000 ha of mountain, forest and tussock grassland.

The Kaweka Forest Park borders the Kaimanawa Forest Park on its eastern boundary and lies west of Hawke's Bay. Its terrain is similar to the Kaimanawas and it covers 67 000 ha.

Climate This is rugged mountainous country and unpredictable weather changes are common. From December to April, the weather is usually mild. However, rain, sleet and snow can occur at any time of the year. The average rainfall is more than 2540 mm. The Parks are noted for their irregular, broken terrain, and because of these features and the climatic conditions, anglers intending to spend time in these Parks would be well advised to carry survival-type equipment. A detailed map is essential.

Kaimanawa Forest Park

Access
- From S.H.5 (the Napier–Taupo road) via Clement's Access Road. A 5 to 7 hour tramp over Te Iringa Saddle to the Oamaru hut. Clement's Access Road is an hour's drive from Taupo.
- From S.H.1 south of Turangi. There are three access roads running in an easterly direction to the Park.
- North from the Taihape–Napier road across private land.
- From forestry roads up the Hinemaia, Tauranga–Taupo and Waimarino rivers.
- By fixed-wing aircraft to various strips, notably the Boyd.
- By helicopter.

Rivers draining into Lake Taupo

Waipakahi River

Does not carry a large fish population because of an unstable shingle bed. There are resident rainbows in the lower reaches which will succumb to a well-presented lure, nymph or spinner. The Waikato Falls and hydro-electric power scheme prevent trout running up river from the Tongariro. The gin-clear mountain water enables fish to be easily spotted.

Tauranga–Taupo River

(See Taupo section for lower reaches.)

Below the falls only 5 km of water lie within the Park boundary. This provides good rainbow fishing. Above the falls there are no trout.

Hatepe or Hinemaiaia River

(See Taupo section for lower reaches.)

The lower hydro-electric dam blocks fish. This dam contains rainbow and brown trout. The upper dam holds Fontinalis or Brook trout which can be caught on a wet fly or spoon. These fish do not fight well but can weigh up to 2 kg. Loose pumice makes wading hazardous in this lake, which can be reached via the Hatepe hydro road south of Taupo airport.

Waimarino River

(See Taupo section.)

This is a spawning stream in the upper reaches and trout can run up only as far as the falls in the vicinity of the Te Pahatu trig station.

Waitahanui River

(See Taupo section.)

Rises from springs in the northern area of the Park. The river is virtually unfishable, being deep, swift and overgrown in its upper reaches.

Rivers draining in a southerly direction

Rangitikei River

(See Wellington District for middle and lower reaches south of the Taihape–Napier road.)

This valley is very exposed to the south, and cold in winter. The river has many deep pools and holds rainbows up to 7.5 kg in crystal-clear water. It is the river to visit for trophy fish. However, hooking one is not easy as the trout tend to lie towards the tail of pools in deep water and are easily frightened. Occasionally in high summer, fish feed on the edge of a run and can be stalked with a dry fly or nymph on a long trace. They will accept a Red Setter, Orange Rabbit, Parson's Glory or a Hairy Dog on a high density line fished downstream. A well-weighted Hair and Copper nymph fished in similar fashion can also be effective on a 2.5–3 m trace.

Location   Source east of Turangi. Flows in a southerly direction to the Taihape–Napier road.

Access   Difficult without a helicopter. It is a rigorous 2-day tramp over Umikarikari and Middle Range. Can be approached from the south over private land, but even this is a difficult 3-hour journey by four wheel drive vehicle. The river crosses the Taihape–Napier road, but this section is outside the Park and is described in the Wellington section.

Mangamaire River

This is the largest tributary of the upper Rangitikei and even more inaccessible. Fishing methods are the same as for the main river. The lower 6 km flows through bush. Above this, the river meanders through a long

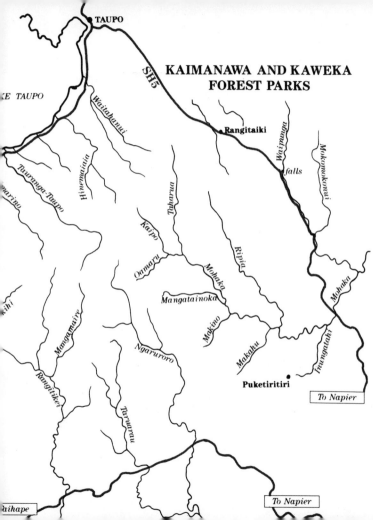

KAIMANAWA AND KAWEKA FOREST PARKS

tussock valley which can be very hot to tramp down in summer. Fish can be spotted and there are some very deep pools providing good stable water. Can be reached from the Boyd Hut after a long day's tramp.

Ngaruroro River

(See Hawke's Bay District for lower reaches.)

Similar to the Rangitikei but flows through open tussock country in the upper reaches. Enters beech bush 14 km downstream from the Boyd. The river is not as large and is easier to fish. A careful approach is essential for success. Although fish are present near the Boyd Hut up and into North Arm, better fishing begins 5 km downstream near Panoko (Gold) Creek.

Location Flows roughly parallel to, but east of, the Rangitikei as far south as the Taihape–Napier road at Kuripapango, where it turns in an easterly direction to flow out through Hawke's Bay.

Access
● A six-hour tramp up the Oamaru Valley from the Oamaru hut. There is an airstrip at the Oamaru.
● At Kuripapango on the Taihape–Napier road.
● By fixed wing to the Boyd airstrip and hut.

Rainbow up to 4 kg can be expected and methods are similar to those described for the Rangitikei. Spinning can also take fish. The river is used for rafting from the Boyd airstrip down to Kuripapango.

Changing a nymph, Oamaru River.

Taururau River

This is the largest tributary of the Ngaruroro River, but access is difficult as the greater part of its course is through private land. The Taihape–Napier road crosses it but gorges limit the fishing water both upstream and downstream. Tramping experience is required to reach the river via the Comet Range south of the Taihape–Napier road. Holds rainbow averaging around 2 kg in clear pools and runs.

Rivers draining in an easterly direction

Mohaka River and its tributaries

(See Hawke's Bay District for middle and lower reaches of the Mohaka.)

Location Three main rivers join to form the Upper Mohaka; the Oamaru and Kaipo drain the bush-clad hills of the Kaimanawa Ranges, while the Taharua rises from springs on the pumice plateau just south of S.H.5 and flows sedately through the farmland of Poronui Station.

Oamaru River

The Oamaru Valley saddles with the upper Ngaruroro 5 km from the Boyd hut. The valley and stream run in a north-easterly direction to join the Kaipo River at the Oamaru Hut.

Above the Oamaru hut, only the first 2–3 km are worth fishing. Below the hut to the confluence with the Taharua, there is excellent water. Fish can be easily spotted and stalked but a careful approach is essential. Brown trout predominate but an occasional rainbow will enliven proceedings. Fish up to 3 kg are present and can be taken on dry fly, nymph, downstream lure or spinner. Care is required when wading as the scalloped-out rocky channels are slippery and treacherous. The river seldom discolours even during a fresh, and returns to normal in 24 hours.

Access
- A 5 to 7-hour tramp over Te Iringa Saddle from Clement's Access Road.
- By fixed wing to the Oamaru strip.
- A 5 to 6-hour tramp from the Boyd Hut and airstrip.
- Private access through Poronui Station.

Kaipo River

Small bush stream rising near Te Iringa Saddle. Contains browns in the lower reaches near the Oamaru hut but overhanging trees present a challenge to the fly angler. A Coch-y-bondhu dry fly or a small Pheasant Tail nymph on a long tippet can be most effective, provided the encroaching vegetation can be avoided.

Taharua River

A clear stream meandering through farmland with patches of manuka scrub along stable banks. Has a pumice and weed bed and contains only brown trout, as fish cannot negotiate the falls near the Mohaka junction. Trout population is self-sustaining. Can flood and become discoloured taking 2–3 days to clear. Fish average 1–2 kg, and rise well to a Coch-y-bondhu or Greenwell's Glory in November and December during

---

Location Rises from springs on the pumice plateau south of the Taupo–Napier road (S.H.5) and flows south through Poronui Station to join the Oamaru River and form the Mohaka.

Access By permission of the landowner at Poronui Station.

---

the green beetle hatch or to a Twilight Beauty in the evening. During the day, fish can be stalked and taken on a small Hair and Copper or Pheasant Tail nymph. This is a classic fly stream, but strong downstream winds often make fly fishing difficult in this open valley.

Mangatainoka River

There is excellent brown trout fishing in the lower river but there are no fish above the falls which are 3–4 km upstream. Dense bush overhangs the stream, providing an abundance of insect life. Trout can be easily spotted and the river is safe to wade.

The Makino and the Makahu are two smaller tributaries downstream from the Mangatainoka. The Makino is not recommended but the Makahu holds trout although it floods readily.

> **Location** Like the Ngaruroro and Oamaru rivers, the Mangatainoka River flows through both the Kaimanawa and Kaweka Forest Parks. It flows in an easterly direction and meets the Mohaka about 6 km upstream from the road end at the Pakaututu Thermal Springs reserve.
>
> **Access** As above.

Upper Mohaka River

This river is for the adventurous angler, and is best combined with tramping or rafting. The river runs in a terraced valley of tussock, impenetrable manuka scrub and clumps of beech trees. Crossings can be hazardous in places. It is truly a wild and scenic river and offers excellent fishing for both fly and spinner. Browns averaging 2–3 kg are plentiful and an occasional rainbow of similar size adds to the attraction.

> **Location** Flows in a south-easterly direction from the Oamaru–Taharua confluence for over 20 km before meeting the Ripia River near Pukaututu. (See Hawke's Bay District.)
>
> **Access**
> - As for the Oamaru and Taharua rivers.
> - From Pakaututu north of Puketitiri.
> - From Otupua airstrip.

Ripia River

Although this river lies outside the Park boundaries, it is convenient to deal with it in this section.

The river was badly affected by a massive flood in

1981 but is slowly recovering. A pleasant river to fish, easy to cross and holds brown and rainbow trout, the former predominating. Fish can be spotted and stalked in clear pools and runs. Flows through tussock, scrub and native bush, especially in the upper reaches.

Location   Source is on Lochinvar Station. Flows in a south-easterly direction to join the Mohaka below the Pukaututu road.

Access   From the Pukaututu road, or with permission of the Forestry Corporation, from S.H.5.

Season   Open season from 1 October — 30 September.

Waipunga River

Above the falls, there are good brown trout in very clear water that will test any dry fly or nymph expert. Wading can be treacherous on the slippery rocks, and a downstream wind needs to be avoided in this open tussock valley.

Below the falls, there is good water holding rainbows up to 4 kg. These can be taken on a weighted nymph fished upstream or a lure fished downstream on a sinking line. An evening rise occurs in some of the quieter pools, and as the valley is bush clad, more shelter is possible than above the falls. The river below the falls is more boisterous and best fished in boots and shorts.

A tributary of the Waipunga, the Mokomokonui River, holds rainbows but access is limited through private land.

Location   This river also lies north of the Park boundaries. Its source is near the Wheao headwaters. Flows in a southerly direction to meet the Taupo–Napier road (S.H.5), 15 km east of Rangitaiki. It follows S.H.5 for 20 km before turning east, south of Tarawera and joining the Mohaka.

Access
Above the falls   Turn off on the Pohokura road, where the river meets S.H.5. Cross one bridge above the falls and turn left. The forestry road follows upstream on the true left bank often some distance from the river.
Below the falls   From S.H.5.

Season   Open 1 October — 30 September.

Note   All the rivers described in this section traverse highly regarded deer country. Anglers are advised to wear at least one item of bright clothing.

Waimarino District

This sparsely populated district is bounded by Taumarunui in the north, Ohakune and Raetihi in the south, Whanganui National Park in the west and Tongariro National Park in the east. Many of the rivers originate from the melting snows of the three volcanoes, Ruapehu, Tongariro and Ngauruhoe. The district offers unlimited opportunity for exciting fishing in a wide variety of water. Apart from tributaries of the Whangaehu River all the other streams described are feeders of the Wanganui River.

Licence The Wanganui River and tributaries can be fished with a Rotorua or an Auckland licence.

Season Open season from 1 July to 30 June on the Wanganui River where it bounds the Auckland Acclimatisation Society's district up to the confluence with the Whakapapa River, and Lake Rotokuru at Kariori. All other waters, 1 October — 30 June.

Whakapapa River

Before water draw-off for hydro development, this was an outstanding fishery. There is still good fishing, however, for both brown and rainbow trout, but the water temperature with the reduction in flow during summer can be marginal for trout.

The headwater tributaries, Whakapapanui and Whakapapaiti, hold only a few fish in very clear water. I explored below the Matariki Falls and upstream from the intake in 1986 and only saw one rainbow. The fish are usually a good size. Below the intake, there is very little water flow until the Otamawairua Stream joins. East of Oio, the river holds reasonable stocks of fish up to 4 kg. The river needs to be fished in boots and shorts. There are some difficult crossings but trout can be spotted in deep clear pools. The scenery is most attractive, with gorges, steep cliffs, native bush and blue ducks.

Upstream from Kakahi, there is still good water with deep pools against bluffs and turbulent runs.

All **legal fishing** methods take fish. Try Mole fly,

Coch-y-bondhu, Kakahi Queen and Twilight Beauty dry flies, Hamill's Killer and Mrs Simpson lures, any weighted nymph in sizes 12–14, and Black and Silver Toby. The Twilight Beauty and Kakahi Queen were created by Mr Basil Humphries, postmaster at Kakahi.

Location   Rises on Mt Ruapehu above the Chateau and joins the Wanganui near Kakahi.

Access
● To the two headwater tributaries, Whakapapanui and Whakapapaiti, which join 2 km west of S.H.47 (the Turangi–National Park road): From S.H.47 by walking downstream or from a hydro road leading to the intake structure for Lake Otamangakau.
● To the main river: From an old timber company road at Owhango or Te Rena Road at Kakahi.
● Across private farmland east of S.H.4 north of Oio. Access is difficult south of Oio because of gorges and cliffs.

Wanganui River

The headwaters provide rugged rock and stone type fishing, whereas in the vicinity of Bennet's Bridge, the river is more sedate, flowing through farmland. There

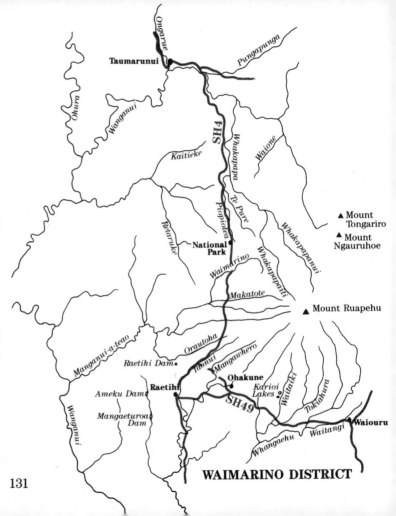

WAIMARINO DISTRICT

Location   Rises on Mt Ruapehu and flows through rough, gorgey bush-clad country until it reaches Bennet's Bridge upstream from Kakahi and the Whakapapa confluence. Becomes a large river below Kakahi and the water quality deteriorates after the Ongarue joins at Taumarunui. The river enters the Whanganui National Park below Taumarunui and once again becomes gorgey, with steep bush-clad cliffs protecting the river. Some 220 km from its source, the river enters the Tasman Sea at Wanganui.

Access
● By four wheel drive vehicle or trail bike over old, rough logging roads from S.H.47 south of Lake Otamangakau. Local knowledge is required.
● From S.H.41 (Taumarunui–Turangi road) 8 km east of Mananui. Turn right on an unsealed road marked Hohotaka. An attractive section of river is reached 7 km along this road.
● From Kakahi, from S.H.4 at Mananui and Piriaka.
● Below Taumarunui, roads follow down each bank.

are excellent pools and runs and the river bed is stoney with occasional outcrops of papa. Willows and native trees line the banks. For 15 km downstream from Taumarunui the river is large, the water brownish in colour and best suited to spinning.

Both brown and rainbow averaging 1.5 kg are present and can be taken on dry fly in the evening, wet fly, weighted nymphs, lure and spinner.

Suggested patterns include Rabbit flies, Parson's Glory, Hamill's Killer and Mrs Simpson lures; Hardy's Favourite and March Brown wet flies; Coch-y-bondhu, Twilight Beauty and Kakahi Queen dry flies; Pheasant Tail, Hare and Copper and Half Back nymphs; Black Toby, Red Veltic and Daffy spinners.

Piopiotea Stream

The first 6 km from National Park lacks good holding water, is small and runs through steep bush-clad country. Below the falls near Raurimu, the stream follows a gentle course across farmland. The stream bed contains boulders, sand, mudstone and silt, while the banks are willow lined. Contains both rainbow and brown trout averaging 1.25 kg. Best fishing is before the end of December when water flows are consistent.

Dry fly and nymph account for most of the fish. Favoured patterns include Coch-y-bondhu and

Twilight Beauty dry flies, and Hare and Copper and Pheasant Tail nymphs.

A tributary of the Piopiotea, the Te Pure Stream, offers 4 km of similar fishing. Access is from Manson's Siding bridge and a shingle road which follows the stream for a short distance along the main trunk railway line. I walked this river for 2 km in December recently, but did not spot a fish, so stocks appear to be low at that time of the year.

Location   Rises near National Park, flows in a northerly direction parallel to, but east of, S.H.4 to join the Whakapapa River at Hukapapa.

Access   Across private farmland from S.H.4 between Raurimu and Oio.

Retaruke and Kaitieke Rivers

From the confluence downstream, there is 20 km of water best suited to spinning. Upstream, the Retaruke offers 8 km of pools and runs while the Kaitieke offers 3 km of similar water until the river gorges. As these rivers drain old volcanic mud flows, the water colour resembles pale home brew and tends to silt easily after a fresh. Despite this, brown trout average 1–2 kg. Some larger fish are occasionally taken. On my visit in January 1988, there had been very little rain, but the Retaruke was heavily silt-laden and unfishable. Apparently, a substantial mud slip into the river had occurred recently. I walked the Kaitieke for approximately 2 km and did not spot a fish. Trout food is predominantly caddis and mayfly larvae. Recommended dry flies are Twilight Beauty and Kakahi Queen; wet flies are March Brown and Black Gnat; nymphs are Pheasant Tail and Hare and Copper; lures are Orange Rabbit, Hamill's Killer and Hairy Dog after dark; spinners are Veltic, Meps and Black Toby especially after a fresh.

Location   Both these rivers rise on the Central Plateau west of National Park and flow in a westerly direction to enter the Wanganui River at Retaruke.

Access   From S.H.4 at Owhango, take the sealed road marked Whakahora, Kaitieke. The confluence of the two rivers is reached after 15 km. From this point, there is a choice of fishing either river from roads following upstream. Permission should be obtained before crossing private farmland.

Manganui-a-te-Ao River

The upper part of this river cuts through deep bush-covered gorges which are not easy to fish. There is good road access lower down to 15 km of water with deep pools and riffles. The water is clear but fish are not easily spotted. Both brown and rainbow up to 3 kg are present, although the average weight is more in the region of 1.5 kg. This is heavy water, although crossings can be made at the tail of most pools. Use a stick for support as the stoney river bed can be slippery. The river is very scenic with some excellent picnic areas. There is always a chance of spotting Blue Ducks as the river is renowned for these birds.

Location   Along with its three feeder streams, the Waimarino, Makatote and Mangaturuturu, this river rises from the slopes of Mt Ruapehu and flows in a westerly direction to join the Wanganui west of Raetihi.

Access   Turn west off S.H.4 about 4 km north of Raetihi on the Ohura road. This road has three branches. The Makakahi road leads to the lower reaches, the Ruatiti road to the middle reaches and the Ruatiti Domain, while the Pukekaha Road gives access to the upper reaches.

Favoured flies include weighted Half Back, Hare and Copper and Caddis nymphs, Coch-y-bondhu and Dad's Favourite dry flies, Hamill's Killer and Mrs Simpson lures fished deep. The spin angler should try Veltics, Meps and the darker Toby lures.

The Waimarino offers attractive water alongside S.H.4 at Waikune, but lower downstream on the Erua Road the river is overgrown and very difficult to fish. The Makatote can be reached from below the Makatote Viaduct, but this is definitely adventurous water, best fished in a wet suit with a float tube.

Orautoha Stream

The upper reaches are small but the lower 5 km are swelled by water entering from the Raetihi hydro dam. Holds mainly browns, up to 2 kg, in pools and runs. The water is brownish and fish are difficult to spot unless rising in a still pool. Provides good dry fly and nymph water. Wading is tricky on the slimy stones.

Location   Rises near S.H.4, flows parallel to the Ohura road and joins the Manganui-a-te-Ao close to the Pukekaha turn-off.

Access   From the Ohura road, across farmland.

Taonui River

The river holds fish throughout its length of 8 km, but is fished mostly in the 4 km below the railway line, where scrub gives way to farmland. Fishing is difficult in the upper reaches due to the manuka and ponga lining the banks. Across the farmland the river is a delight to fish, flowing over a rock and gravel bed with long runs and occasional deep pools. Patches of native bush and a few willows present few problems on the backcast. Holds mainly browns averaging 0.75–2 kg, with the odd fish up to 4 kg. Trout can be spotted and stocks are good. During the day, fish are very shy. Best fished with nymph or dry fly. Favoured patterns include weighted Half Back, Hare and Copper, Caddis and Pheasant Tail nymphs in sizes 12–14, Coch-y-bondhu, Red Palmer, Twilight Beauty and Kakahi Queen dry flies.

Location Rises from springs on the lower slopes of Ruapehu between Ohakune and Horopito. Flows in a south-westerly direction to join the Mangawhero River halfway between Ohakune and Raetihi.

Access From S.H.49A and from Old Mangarewa Road near the Mangawhero confluence.

Mangawhero River

Fishing is difficult in the National Park due to overhanging native bush and scrub. Downstream from the Ohakune Ranger Station there are 10 km of water flowing across farmland before the river leaves the Central Plateau and enters a gorge. This stretch above the gorge offers pools, rocky runs and placid willow-lined reaches. The water has a brownish tinge and

Location Rises on the southern slopes of Mt Ruapehu, flows 70 km through Ohakune in a southerly direction to join the Whangaehu River near Kauangaroa.

Access
● From the Turoa Skifield road in the Tongariro National Park.
● The river leaves the Park at the Ohakune Ranger Station and flows through the borough of Ohakune. Access from Old Mangarewa Road, S.H.49, and Pakahi Road. Permission is required to cross private farmland.
● From the Parapara highway, S.H.4 is also possible.

Licence The upper 40 km of river are in the Rotorua District. Below this a Wanganui licence is required.

becomes silt-laden rapidly after a fresh. However, there is reasonable fly fishing in this stretch.

The river emerges from its gorge on the Parapara Highway (S.H.4) and offers another 15 km of fishable water above and below the falls at Kakatahi. The river holds mainly browns averaging 1.5 kg. Below the falls, the river is large and holds good stocks of fish. These tend to seek shelter in deep rock crevices and are not readily visible. They can be fished with weighted nymphs, large dry flies or spinners.

Favoured flies as for the Taonui River along with Meps, Veltic and Black Toby spinners.

Tokiahuru River

Fast-flowing cold clear mountain water holding strong rainbow and brown trout averaging 2 kg. This river often remains fishable when neighbouring streams are discoloured after a fresh. Forest gives way to farmland at the railway line and fishing is generally more profitable in the 10 km below this point before the river joins the Whangaehu. However, a chainsaw in the backpack could come in handy. The banks are overgrown with manuka, and fly fishing is very difficult except in a few selected spots.

Trout food consists of caddis, koura, mayflies and creeper. Best fished from the end of November and with heavily weighted size 10–12 nymphs.

Location   Rises from springs and snow-fed water in the Karioi State Forest on the south-eastern slopes of Ruapehu. Flows in a south-westerly direction to join the Whangaehu River south of Karioi.

Access
● *Upper river*   Forestry Corporation headquarters on S.H.49.
● *Lower river*   Whangaehu Valley Road. Flows alongside the Kariori Domain.

Waitaiki River

Similar fast-flowing river to the Tokiahuru, and heavily weighted nymphs on 4 kg nylon are needed for success. Apart from a few stretches across farmland, the banks are thick with scrub and the river choked with willows. Fish are in excellent condition after November, and fight well. The Whangaehu River is polluted from Mt Ruapehu's crater lake so the Tokiahuru and Waitaiki rivers are isolated from waters further downstream. There are other small tributaries of the Whangaehu holding fish. Waitangi Stream, flowing alongside S.H.49 between Tangiwai and Waiouru, is worth investigating.

> **Location**   Flows in a similar direction, parallel to, but west of, the Tokiahuru River and joins this river 4 km above the Whangaehu confluence south of Karioi.
>
> **Access**   From Karioi Station Road and Whangaehu Valley Road.

Raetihi Hydro Dam

Fly fishing only on this small, 1 ha lake. Holds browns averaging 1 kg which are difficult to take during the day unless a small sunk nymph is used. Pine trees surround the lake, and deep wading is required to clear the backcast unless one fishes off the lip of the dam. On warm summer evenings there is often a good rise to caddis and Thompson's Moth is a favourite pattern. Other sedge imitations such as Twilight Beauty, Pye's

> **Location and access**   Turn west off S.H.4 on the Ohuru road, 4 km north of Raetihi, then turn right after 2 km on Middle Road. Travel 750 m and turn left onto a rough track leading to the dam and power station.

Sedge and Turkey Sedge can be equally effective. Trout can be seen cruising the shoreline during the day.

Karioi Lakes

The lakes cover 10 ha, and because of dense marginal vegetation are difficult to fish unless a light dinghy or inflatable is carried up the track or spinning gear used. A float tube would be equally effective. Although the lakes are only 200 m apart, they differ markedly from each other. The top lake (Rotokuru) is a flooded volcanic crater, heavily bushed and very deep. The bottom lake is shallow with the margins covered in raupo. Both hold rainbow in the 0.5–1 kg range. Although no smelt or bullies inhabit the lakes, spin anglers take fish on red, black and green Toby and Veltic lures. I watched a fish in the lower lake leap 2 m

> **Location and access**   Turn off S.H.49 about 10 km south-east of Ohakune at a road signposted Karioi Railway Station. Cross the railway line and travel 1 km to a parking area signposted Lake Rotokura Ecological Reserve. A 10-minute walk through native bush brings you to the lakes.
>
> **Season**   There is an open season on both lakes from 1 October to 30 September.

out of the water to take a Damsel fly. For the fly fisher, try Mrs Simpson, Hamill's Killer or Craig's Night-time fished deep. Flies imitating midge pupae, damsel and dragonfly larvae, water boatmen and snails fished in the surface film are also effective. The lakes are best fished in the summer months.

Ameku and Mangaeturoa Dams

These waters are restricted to fly fishing only. Rainbow trout have recently been introduced into these new waters. Fly casting from the shore is unlimited as the banks are grassy in nature. Use similar flies to those described for the Karioi Lakes.

Location and access   These are the Winstone Afforestation dams. A permit is required to enter this forest and can be obtained from Winstone Afforestation Ltd., P.O. Box 129, Queen Street, Raetihi (Phone 54-111). Turn off the Raetihi-Pipiriki road 5 km from Raetihi at a sign marked Mangaeturoa North. Travel 7.5 km to an access road marked Tirau Road. The Ameku Dam is 2 km beyond the locked gate. The Mangaeturoa Dam is a further 5 km along Mangaeturoa North Road.

There are a number of other smaller feeder streams in the Waimarino District that hold good fish and are well worth exploring. Some, such as the Waimarino and Makatote, run in very deep gorges, but offer exciting fishing for the active and experienced back country angler who does not mind swimming through some of the pools. The Wanganui tributaries north of Taumarunui are described in the King Country section.

Taranaki, Stratford and Hawera Districts

Many streams drain the high rainfall and melting snows from Mt Taranaki. Most have short, steep courses and fluctuating water flow rates. The headwaters tend to be rocky and rough, while the middle and lower reaches traverse highly productive dairy farms. Streams have deteriorated as a result of scrub and bush clearance, enrichment from fertilisers, cowshed and dairy factory effluent, land drainage and, in the case of the Kapuni River, petrochemical poisoning. Some rivers are even used by farmers to dispose of their refuse. Four streams have been dammed for electricity generation. Many long-term residents and anglers speak wistfully of bygone days when limit bags of good-sized brown trout taken on opening day were quite common.

Another theory to explain reduced stocks concerns the use of ova boxes for restocking streams. Some local anglers claim that eels suck out the ova. Apparently they also enjoy fry, and the locals maintain that fingerling liberation is the only successful method.

However, streams will only support a limited number of fish and when streams are over-stocked, many will retreat to the sea during unfavourable conditions. It has been suggested that fingerlings bred from fish that never leave a river be used. Such brown trout parent stock can be found in the Taharua River above the falls and, in the case of rainbow, in the Ruakaturi River above the Waitangi Falls.

Unfortunately, though, it seems the problem is more complex. Water quality must be improved and perhaps a limit bag of two fish should be introduced to give resident fish the chance to breed in order to restock the streams with their own progeny.

All streams carry limited stocks of brown trout. The Stony (Hangatahua) is the exception in holding rainbow. The streams are a delight to fish, being well served by a network of roads, and most farmers are generous in allowing access provided permission is sought beforehand.

This district is unique in that live bait fishing with

creeper is permitted in most waters and this method remains the most popular. Creepers, which are larvae of the Dobson fly, are found under rocks at the edge of streams. They are attached to a size 10 or 12 hook and caste upstream with a fly rod in similar fashion to nymph fishing. The strike is similar but somewhat slower than a nymph. Creeper is excellent bait at the beginning of the season, but not so effective in the warm summer months when streams are low and clear. Dry fly and nymph fishing are also popular, although fish can be taken on small wet flies and spinning gear.

Weather conditions dictate when fly fishing is possible and as strong westerlies predominate during spring and early summer, it is wise to check before setting out for a day's enjoyment. Shelter and an upstream breeze are desirable when dry fly fishing.

Season   Unless otherwise stated, 1 October — 3 April. In the Hawera Acclimatisation District the season is closed from 21 to 30 April.

Lake Mangamahoe

This lake has been created for power generation by the damming of the Mangamahoe Stream.

This is a beautiful setting and grand picnic spot. It

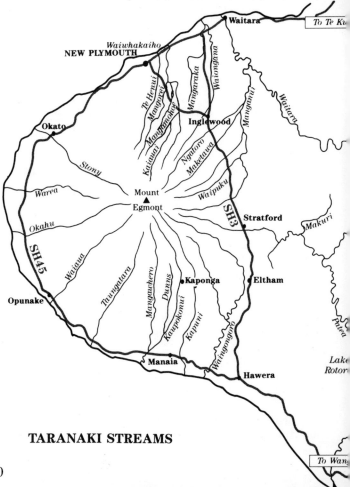

TARANAKI STREAMS

140

is a wildlife refuge holding varieties of water fowl. Brown and rainbow are present. Fish can sometimes be spotted. A small nymph during the day or a Cochy-bondhu dry fly in December–February when the beetles hatch can be effective. At night use a size 4–6 Hairy Dog or a Fuzzy Wuzzy. It is rarely necessary to wade.

Location   Turn-off is well marked on the New Plymouth–Inglewood road before Egmont Village.

Restrictions   Fly fishing only.

Season   1 October — 30 April and 1 June — 30 September. May is the duck-shooting season.

Access   Road skirts western shore.

Waiwhakaiho River and tributaries

A delightful stream to fish. An occasional rainbow has been taken, but browns in the 0.5-1.5 kg range are expected. Fly creeper and spinner are equally effective.

Recommended tributaries are the Kaiauai and the Mangawara. The Kaiauai joins the Waiwhakaiho 1.5 km up Alfred Road. Both provide pleasant small stream

fishing, although fish stocks have deteriorated in recent times. Some deep holding pools are present.

Location   Drains from Mt Taranaki and flows in a northerly direction close to New Plymouth.

Access   Middle reaches are crossed by the New Plymouth–Inglewood road just beyond the Lake Mangamahoe turn-off. Upper reaches from Alfred Road near the New Plymouth Gliding Club.

Season   Downstream from the main road bridge at Fitzroy, there is a winter season from 10 June to 30 September. Elsewhere, 1 October — 30 April.

Waiongana Stream

Middle reaches near Lepperton are favoured, live bait and spinner being most popular. Brown trout in the 0.5–1 kg range.

Location   Enters the sea just south of Waitara. Crossed by S.H.3. The upper reaches flow through the outskirts of Inglewood.

Te Henui Stream

Small stream holding browns up to 0.75 kg. An ideal stream for junior anglers.

> **Location**   Flows through New Plymouth.

Stony River (Hangatahua)

Highly valued by local anglers. Contains rainbow and brown trout. There are some large sea-run browns in very deep holes in the lower reaches. These can be taken on heavily weighted nymphs fished Tongariro style. The water is extremely clear in this river and fish can be spotted in the middle and upper reaches. The clean river bed provides safe wading. Fly, spinner and live bait are equally effective. The river has been subjected to severe flooding in the past, but has recovered well.

> **Location and access**   Crosses the New Plymouth–Opunake road (S.H.45) just south of Okato.
> *Lower reaches*   Kaihihi and Brophy Roads — turn off at Okato Tavern.
> *Middle reaches*   Via New Zealand Walkway System opposite Okato domain.
> *Upper reaches*   Off Wiremu Road.
>
> **Season**   Below S.H.45 there is a winter season from 10 June to 30 September.

Warea River

This is a productive little stream holding browns up to 1.5 kg. Nymph or creeper is preferred.

> **Location**   South of Okato and the Stony River.
>
> **Access**   Large stretch of fishable water from Warea Road, which runs parallel to the river.

Okahu River

Clear water similar to the Stony but holds browns.

> **Location**   Crosses S.H.45, south of Rahotu.
>
> **Access**   Off Ngariki Road.

Waiaua River

The lower reaches hold many small browns and are fun to fish with a small nymph or dry fly. Early in the season, creeper is effective.

Location Lower reaches flow by Opunake and are dammed for power generation.

Access From Ihaia Road. Large area of accessible water.

Season Downstream from the main road bridge at Opunake there is a winter season from 10 June to 30 September. Elsewhere, 1 October — 30 April.

Kapuni River

A pleasant river to fish but although fish stocks are reasonable, trout tend to be small. Has suffered badly in the past from petrochemical pollution.

Location Flows south, just east of Kaponga, to enter the sea near Manaia.

Access From the Stratford–Opunake road or the Eltham–Opunake road.

Kaupokonui and tributaries

This river and its two tributaries, Dunn's Creek and the Mangawhero Stream, offer good dry fly, nymph, and creeper fishing for browns up to 2 kg. Popular with local anglers.

Location Flows in a southerly direction just west of Kaponga and Manaia.

Access From the Stratford–Opunake road.

Season Winter season downstream from South Road. 10 June — 30 September. Elsewhere, 1 October — 30 April.

Patea River

Limited stocks of small brown trout but water quality is not great. The lower end of this river has been dammed and now forms Lake Rotorangi.

Location Flows through Stratford, south of Toko and then turns south to enter the sea at Patea.

Access Reasonable in the upper reaches near Stratford.

Waingongoro River, Taranaki.

Waingongoro River

Large stretches of good water, but some areas are overgrown by willows. The middle reaches south of Eltham are most favoured as there are some very deep holes. All methods bring success and browns up to 1.5 kg can be expected. One of the more favoured Taranaki rivers.

Location   Runs parallel to, but west of, the Stratford–Hawera highway (S.H.3).

Access   From side roads off S.H.3, often across private farms.

Season   Winter season, 10 June — 30 September, downstream from South Road.

Lake Rotorangi

This lake is fishing very well. Mainly rainbow trout in good condition can be caught from a boat harling a fly or trolling a spinner. The lake is 49 km long but very narrow. There is considerable bush cover on the banks.

Manganui River and tributaries

Good water flowing through farmland with patches of native bush on one side or the other. Highly favoured by local anglers and fish stocks are reasonable. Creeper are commonly used in the deep holes although nymph and dry fly are more effective in the warmer summer months.

Location   Flows in a northerly direction parallel to but east of S.H.3 and 3 km from Midhurst to Inglewood to join the Waitara River east of Lepperton.

Access   Turn off at Tariki and travel 4 km down the Tariki road to the bridge just above the Power Board dam. This is private access and permission must be obtained to fish.

Three kilometres upstream from the bridge on Tariki Road, the Waipuku Stream enters. This also has some deep holes holding fish. S.H.3 crosses this stream south of Tariki. Two other favoured feeder streams are crossed by S.H.3, the Ngatoro 4 km south of Inglewood and the Maketawa 8 km south of Inglewood. Fish up to 1.5 kg are not uncommon.

Many other smaller streams flowing off Mt Taranaki hold small brown trout. The countryside is attractive and in clear weather views of the mountain are quite spectacular. There are a number of small lakes and dams in these districts holding trout and perch, but apart from the larger lakes Mangamohoe and Rotorangi these are not recommended.

The rivers between Hawera and Wanganui do not hold trout.

Wellington District

There are three main river systems in this large district. In the north is the Rangitikei River rising in the Kaimanawa Forest Park. The upper reaches lying in the Rotorua District are described in the Kaimanawa section. In the south is the Ruamahanga and its tributaries. Between these two river systems is the Manawatu River and its numerous feeder streams draining northern Wairarapa and southern Hawke's Bay. Many of the rivers rise in the high rainfall bush-clad Tararua and Ruahine Ranges.

Brown trout were first introduced in 1874, and rainbow trout around 1898 although these are now only present in the Rangitikei River, having not become established elsewhere.

Season Unless otherwise stated, from 1 October to 30 April. A number of streams in this district have an open season. The bag limit is 12 trout.

Wainuiomata River

Below the main township bridge, fly fishing only is permitted. Because of its proximity to the Hutt Valley and Wellington, this stream is very popular. The headwaters lie in a restricted area due to draw-off for domestic water supply. The most productive water is in the middle and lower reaches 8 km south of Wainuiomata. There are 20 km of slow-flowing fishable water, but the water quality in the lower reaches is often poor.

Despite eroding banks, sewage effluent, eutrophication and weed growth, this river is a most productive fishery. Holds brown trout in the 0.5–2 kg range, but an occasional fish weighing 4 kg has been taken. Best fished early in the season before algae grow in the warmer water. Trout can be spotted in the middle reaches and there is usually an evening rise. The river winds through gorse-covered farmland, but casting is not impeded by vegetation. Beware of the north wind blowing down the valley.

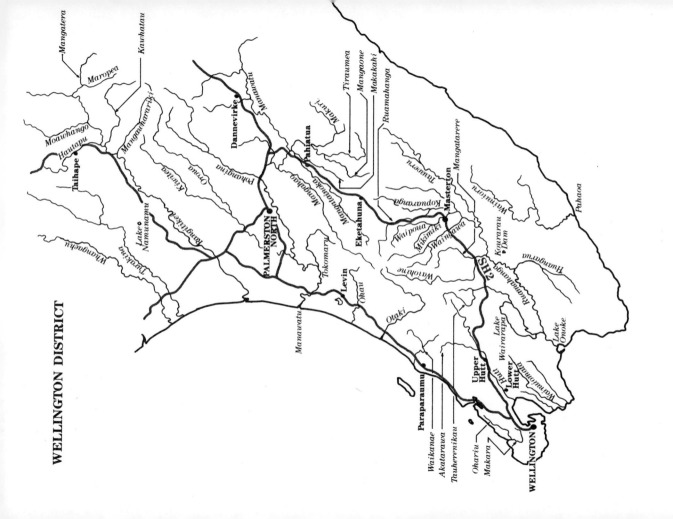

WELLINGTON DISTRICT

Try Dad's Favourite, Red Tipped Governor, Blue Dun and Black Spider dry flies during the day and Twilight Beauty for the evening rise, preferably in sizes 14–16. Small weighted nymphs such as caddis imitations, Half Back and Pheasant Tail will take fish during the day.

Location   Rises in the Rimutaka Range east of Lower Hutt, flows in a southerly direction through Wainuiomata to enter Cook Strait near Baring Head.

Access   The Coast Road follows the Wainuiomata River down the true left bank from Wainuiomata to the mouth.

Hutt River

As it flows through an area of high population density, this river has been subjected to a wide range of pollution. The headwaters are closed for domestic water supply.

The lower 3 km are tidal and although the water in the most heavily fished middle reaches is often not pristine in quality, brown trout can occasionally be spotted. There are well-established pools and runs over a stable shingle bed. Drift dives have confirmed a high fish population in this river especially between the

Akatarawa River confluence and the Silverstream Bridge. Trout average around 0.75 kg, although occasional sea-run browns entering the lower reaches have been caught weighing 4 kg. Fish can be taken on flies and spinners although a sunk nymph fished upstream or a small Taupo-style lure fished downstream usually take most fish. There is no evening rise.

Location   Drains the southern Tararua Ranges and flows in a southerly direction down the Hutt Valley to enter Wellington Harbour near Petone.

Access   Well serviced by roads in the Hutt Valley.

Season   Open season from 1 October to 30 September.

Akatarawa River

This is a small tributary of the Hutt River flowing through scrub, pine plantations and farmland. It holds limited stocks of brown trout and although the fish population is considerably less than in the Hutt River, trout tend to be larger. Access is difficult in parts, but the best fishing is where the river crosses farmland away from gorges. Fish can be stalked and respond to small dry flies and nymphs. Best early in the season before the water becomes warm and weedy.

> **Location and access** Flows in a southerly direction down the Akatarawa Valley to join the Hutt River near Upper Hutt. Access from the Upper Hutt–Waikanae road, which follows up the true left bank.
>
> **Season** 1 October — 30 April. Fly fishing only above the Karapoti road ford.

Other small feeder streams — the Little Akatarawa, Mangaroa and Whatatikei — are nursery streams of the Hutt River and are not recommended.

Makara and Ohariu streams

They are not widely fished but fish better early in the season with small dry flies or nymphs. They both flow through pastoral country and although the Ohariu is gorgey in places with tumbling rapids and pools, the

> **Location** These are two small streams that join before entering the Tasman Sea at Makara Beach, Ohariu Bay, west of Wellington.

water becomes eutrophic from fertiliser run-off during the warmer summer months. Below their confluence, the water becomes slow and sluggish.

Waikanae River

Delightful small clear shingly river offering pleasant dry fly fishing for brown trout in the 0.5–0.75 kg range. Most productive reaches are above the railway bridge and below Reikorangi. The river is very scenic, meandering through patches of rewarewa and tawa. There is some good holding water with stable deep pools against rocky bluffs. Generally holds a good stock of fish, but numbers fluctuate from year to year depending on weather conditions.

> **Location** Flows from the Tararua Ranges in an easterly direction to enter the Tasman Sea at Waikanae Beach.
>
> **Access** From the Waikanae–Upper Hutt road via the Akatarawa Gorge and Reikorangi Road from Waikanae.
>
> **Season** Open from 1 October to 30 September.

Otaki River

Although fish stocks and the catch rate are not high, this river is popular because of the scenic qualities of the bush-clad upper reaches. Below the Forks, pools are large and the deep holding water is more suited to spinning or downstream lure fishing. Rafting is popular on this stretch of river. Fish in the 0.75–1.5 kg range can be taken, especially on a deeply sunk Orange Rabbit or a Mrs Simpson. Fishing the upper reaches is best combined with tramping, but fish numbers are not high. They will respond to a deeply sunk nymph. When the whitebait are running after a fresh from September to November, try a smelt fly in the lower reaches.

Location   Like the Waikanae River further south, the Otaki flows from the Tararuas in an easterly direction to enter the sea near Otaki.

Access   The Otaki Gorge road follows the true left bank to Otaki Forks. The upper reaches can only be reached on foot by tramping in the Tararua Forest Park.

Season   Above the railway bridge, 1 October — 30 April. Below the bridge, open season from 1 October to 30 September.

Ohau River

Occasional estuarine-living or sea-run browns enter this stream. Generally, fishing is better in the lower reaches below S.H.1. Contains small browns although an occasional fish weighing 2–3 kg is taken. The middle reaches have been subjected to gravel extraction. However, the lower reaches offer a stable shingle river bed, clear water and willow-lined banks. Wading is easy although there are some deep pools. Best fished with dry fly or nymph. An evening rise occurs in favourable conditions. Has two small feeder streams, the Makaretu and the Makahika.

Location   Flows east from the Tararuas to enter the sea south of Levin.

Access   Turn off S.H.1 onto Parikawau Road just north of the main road bridge. This leads to a riverside rest area below the bridge.

Season   Open 1 October — 30 September.

u River.

Rangitikei River and tributaries

Rangitikei River (middle and lower reaches)

East of Taihape near Pukeokahu, the river runs deep in a rugged gorge and is difficult to fish. North of this at Mangaohane there are easy pools and runs. There is good water downstream for 10 km from the Taihape–Napier road bridge before the river gorges. There is good access and a campsite in the native bush east of Mangaweka. The river is large and deep in this area and crossings are tricky. Both brown and rainbow are present and good-conditioned fish up to 3 kg are not uncommon. The river has a shingle, rock and papa bed with long pools and riffles.

From Utiku south, the river has carved out an impressive bed. The towering cliffs are easily seen from S.H.1. This more unstable water is best suited to downstream lure and spinning. The best stretch of water lies between Utiku and Bulls. In pools where there are stable conditions and especially where vegetation overhangs the bank, an evening rise can be anticipated.

There is evidence that salmon have spawned in this river. However, the river is not recommended as a salmon fishery.

Location Only the middle and lower reaches are described here, as the upper reaches lie in the Kaimanawa Forest Park. Below the Taihape–Napier road, this major river flows parallel to, but east of, S.H.1 from Taihape to Bulls.

Access This is not difficult as a number of roads either cross the river or follow down the banks.

Season There is an open season downstream from the Mangaohane Bridge 1 October — 30 September. Above the bridge, 1 October — 30 April.

Hautapu River

Fly fishing only above Ngawaka Bridge. The most productive reaches are between Mataroa and Hihitahi. Unfortunately, this river easily becomes silt-laden, but in clear conditions there is excellent brown trout fishing. Fish can be spotted and stalked. Fish up to 2.5 kg are not unusual and dry fly and nymph are equally effective. When the water is low fish are very wary. The only effective method of approach is on all fours. The banks grow patches of native bush, beautiful kowhai and some willows. The main trunk railway follows this valley. I found fish accepted a size 14 or

16 Royal Wulff or a Coch-y-bondhu carefully presented on a long 2 kg tippet. A small Pheasant Tail nymph proved equally effective.

Location Drains the Ngamatea Swamp and southern Kaimanawas south-east of Waiouru. Flows in a southerly direction through Taihape to join the Rangitikei south of Utiku.

Access Turn off S.H.1 about 5 km north of Taihape, west on Mataroa Road to Mataroa. There is river access beneath a railway viaduct at Mataroa. Elsewhere, access is across private farmland. Access is also possible from S.H.1 at Taihape and both north and south of the town.

Turakina River

This river lies in the Wanganui District and is not a tributary of the Rangitikei River. However, it is described in this section as the access to fishing water is via Mataroa from Taihape.

The river flows through unstable papa country and discolours readily after rain. There are patches of bush in reserves along the banks; elsewhere, the stream flows through farmland. Holds a good stock of brown trout that can be taken on similar flies to those described for the Hautapu River (above).

Location   Rises south-west of Waiouru and flows in a southerly direction to eventually enter the sea 25 km south of Wanganui.

Access   Travel to Mataroa off S.H.1 as for the Hautapu River. Then continue for 18 km to Colliers Junction and the upper reaches of the Turakina River.

Season   Open 1 October — 30 September.

Moawhango River

Unfortunately, this once excellent river has suffered greatly from hydro development and reduced water flow. There are fontinalis in the upper reaches and still reasonable stocks of rainbow further downstream. However, fish are not in good condition and the river becomes very sluggish and warm in summer. A careful approach with dry fly or nymph is recommended. The fish are very easily frightened in low water conditions. The evening rise is the time to fish.

Location   Drains the Kaimanawas east of the Desert Road (S.H.1), flows in a southerly direction east of Waiouru and Taihape to join the Rangitikei at Taoroa.

Access   At Moawhango on the Taihape–Napier road, through private farmland north of here. There is also access through Army land east of Waiouru, but permission is not generally granted, and from the Moawhango–Taoroa road.

Season   Open 1 October — 30 September.

Whakaurekou, Maropea, Mangatera, Kawhatau and Mangawharariki rivers

These rivers all drain the Ruahine Ranges east of Mangaweka. At times they contain fish, but flooding, shifting shingle and an unstable bed do not provide a good environment for trout. (The Kawhatau is a spawning stream for the Rangitikei). They are not heavily fished. There is an open season from 1 October to 30 September in the Kawhatau River. Access is generally through private farmland although the headwaters of the Mangatera, Maropea and Kawhatau lie in the Ruahine State Forest Park. The Whakaurekou holds rainbow and is worth fishing with a weighted nymph in November. Access to this river is difficult, however. The Mangawhararariki holds a few good browns.

Lake Namu Namu

This is a very deep lake surrounded by native bush and open to all legal methods of fishing. It is kept stocked with rainbow. Shoreline fishing is difficult but two rowboats owned by the Wellington Acclimatisation Society are available for use. A sunk Taupo-style lure is the most popular method.

Location   Lies west of Hunterville on Ngaruru Station off Turakina Road.

Access   Permission by courtesy of Mr Malcom Thomson. There is a 1-hour walk in.

Season   Open 1 October — 30 September

Manawatu River and tributaries

Manawatu River

Above Dannevirke, there is excellent fly water. The river lies east of S.H.2, and the upper reaches cross this highway just north of Norsewood. Fish can be spotted and stalked with dry fly and nymph and brown trout up to 3 kg are not uncommon. There are good pools and runs through willows and farmland. Eutrophication can cause problems in hot summer conditions. The stretch of water on Oringi Road contains a very high fish population ascertained by drift dives. The river here has a shingle and mud bed with long, large deep pools and wide shingly riffles. Trout are difficult to spot but wading is safe.

Downstream from Woodville, the water is heavy and more suited to wet fly and spinning. Here the river is heavily fished by all legal methods. These include dry and wet fly, nymph, spinner and live bait. More recently, anglers have been employing Taupo techniques using two weighted nymphs or a high density line and lure. Others have been successful with a nymph sunk with the aid of split shot and cast with a spinning rod. The water quality deteriorates at Opiki, and the lower 20 km are tidal.

Alan nymphing a quiet corner of the Upper Manawatu River.

Location   This large popular river drains southern Hawke's Bay, the southern Ruahines and the northern Tararua ranges. The main river follows a southerly course to Dannevirke where it turns east and enters the Manawatu Gorge, 8 km east of Woodville. It emerges from the gorge near Ashhurst, meanders across farmland to Palmerston North and eventually reaches the sea at Foxton Beach.

Access   This is not difficult as roads follow the river quite closely throughout most of its course. Permission is required to cross private farmland. Some suggested roads to take include:
● Kopua Road which leaves S.H.2 just south of the Manawatu bridge between Takapau and Norsewood.
● Garfield Road, 19 km north of Dannevirke, to Makotuku, then on Donghi or Rakaiatai Roads.
● Oringi Road, 10 km south of Dannevirke.

Season   Downstream from Ngawapurua Bridge there is an open season from 1 October to 30 September. Elsewhere, 1 October — 30 April.

Tokomaru Stream

The upper bush-clad reaches hold good fish, but access is across private land and a tramp through gorges is required. Fish tend to be smaller but more numerous where the stream crosses farmland. The river has a shingle bed and can be approached upstream from the railway line. Below the railway the river becomes slow and sluggish.

Location and access   Rises in the Tararuas, flows in an easterly direction and crosses S.H.57 just south of Tokomaru.

Two other small streams, the Kahuterewa and the Tiritea, cross S.H.57 between Linton and Palmerston North. The Kahuterewa is a major spawning stream of the Manawatu and provides good fishing during April before the season closes on 31 April.

Oroua River

This is quite a popular river, with the middle reaches between Kimbolton and Apiti being the most productive. Water quality deteriorates below Feilding due to sewerage and freezing works outfalls. Holds moderate stocks of brown trout in the 0.5–1 kg range. In the upper·bush-clad reaches there are a few good fish which can be spotted and stalked. However, the river has an unstable shingle bed which can change significantly during a flood. Dry flies, nymphs and spinners are all effective in taking fish. The middle reaches are best fished early or late in the season, i.e., October — November and April — May.

Location and access   Rises in the Whanahuia Range, flows in a south-westerly direction parallel to, but east of, the Kiwitea Stream to enter the Manawatu at Opiki. Access from side roads running east off S.H.54 between Feilding, Kimbolton and Apiti.

Season   Open 1 October — 30 September.

Kiwitea Stream

Flows through farmland, holds moderate stocks of small brown trout but is not heavily fished. Has a shingle bed. Best fished in the cooler months.

Location and access   Runs in a south-westerly direction west of Kimbolton and Cheltenham and joins the Oroua Stream near Feilding.

Pohangina River

This is a very scenic river popular for picnicking but fish stocks are not high. Holds browns averaging 0.75 kg. The most productive reaches lie well above the Totara Reserve in the Ruahines, but the upper reaches are prone to shifting shingle and floods. Fish respond equally to small wet and dry flies, nymphs and spinners. Best fished from October to December. Good campsites are available in the Totara Reserve. This river is not highly recommended.

Location   Rises in the Ruahines east of Kimbolton. Follows a south-westerly course down the foothills on the eastern side of the main range and enters the Manawatu at the western end of the gorge.

Access   Turn north at Ashhurst where roads follow upstream on both banks.

Season   Open 1 October — 30 September.

Mangahao River

The upper reaches can only be reached on foot and provide reasonable fly fishing for brown trout in the 0.75–1.5 kg range. Fish can be spotted and stalked, though their numbers are not great. The river below the dam remains clear after a fresh has discoloured neighbouring streams. Fish can be taken on lure, dry fly, nymph and spinner. Trout average 0.75 kg. The willow-lined middle and lower reaches cross farmland.

Location   Rises in the Tararua Ranges and flows in a north-easterly direction to enter the Manawatu River at the eastern end of the gorge south of Woodville. Flows parallel to, but west of, the Mangatainoka River.

Access
- *Upper reaches above the three hydro dams* From the dam access road south-east of Shannon via Mangaore.
- *Lower and middle reaches*   Easy road access off S.H.2 south and west of Pahiatua to Mangahao, Nikau and Marima.

Season   Open season downstream from Marima Reserve Bridge 1 October — 30 September. Above the bridge, 1 October — 30 April.

Mangatainoka River

This river is highly valued by anglers and heavily fished. A conservation order has recently been taken out on it. Fish stocks are good as checked by drift dives. The river bed is shingle and the low willow-lined banks generally permit unobstructed fly casting on one side of the river. Crossings are generally not difficult although the stony bed can be slippery. There are approximately 45 km of fishable water. The middle and lower reaches are the most productive and hold slightly larger fish than the upper reaches. Above Hukanui, the river is more unstable and prone to changing course in floods. There is often a good evening rise, and fish can be spotted and stalked in the middle and upper reaches. Try size 12–14 Pheasant Tail, Half Back, Hare's Ear or Midge Pupa nymphs during the day along with Coch-y-bondhu and Dad's Favourite dry flies. In the evening, it is hard to go past Twilight Beauty in sizes 12–14. Browns in the 0.75–2 kg range can be expected.

Location   Flows parallel to, and between, S.H.2 in the east and the Mangahao River in the west. Enters the Manawatu south of Woodville near Ngawapurua.

Access   Good road access west from S.H.2 at successive turn-offs to Mangamutu at Konini, to Mangamaire and to Hukanui from Hamua. The Mangatainoka Valley road can be reached west of Eketahuna.

Season   Open 1 October — 30 September below the Makakahi confluence. Above this junction, 1 October — 30 April.

Note   Fly fishing only above the road bridge on the Hamua–Hukanui road.

Makakahi River

Pleasant fly stream meandering through farmland and suitable for the dry fly and nymph angler all the way from its confluence with the Mangatainoka to well above Eketahuna in the Tararuas. Use the same flies as recommended for the Mangatainoka. Fish of a similar size can be expected. The most productive stretch of water lies near Hamua. Best fished early in the season before the onset of eutrophication in the warmer summer months. The river bed varies between weed, stone and mud and the banks are willow lined. Wading and crossing in the middle and lower reaches can be tricky. Fish are not easy to spot. Often a good evening rise. Live bait is not permitted.

Makuri River

Fly fishing only is permitted above the township bridge. This is a small tributary of the Tiraumea River and is highly rated by fly anglers. The most popular stretch of water lies in the region of Makuri village where the willow-lined stream wanders across farmland. Trout are easily spotted and just as easily frightened, so a careful approach and fine tippets are essential for success. Fish fight well and have a tendency to tangle in the willow roots. Downstream in the region of the gorge, limestone sink holes and native bush provide considerable interest. Boots and shorts are recommended for this rough piece of water. Good fishing continues for 1 km below the gorge, then the river becomes sluggish and uninteresting. Although anglers consider this river has deteriorated over the past 20 years, drift dives by Acclimatisation Society officers have been reassuring and some excellent fish up to 3 kg have been seen. Due to clear-felling in the headwaters, this river easily becomes silt-laden in a fresh. There is good camping in the Makuri Domain.

Neither the Tiraumea nor Mangaone River is recommended. The Tiraumea is slow and sluggish. Browns can be caught on a spinner.

Kourarau Dam

Covers 11 ha. Contains rainbow trout and perch and is open all season to all legal methods of fishing. Each year, a trout weighing 5 kg is caught, usually on a big black night lure fished from a boat.

Ruamahanga River and tributaries

Ruamahanga River

A popular river with anglers because of the good catch rate, large area of fishable water and easy access. The river has a wide shingle bed, some willows, and near Masterton there are cliffs. The middle reaches are the most heavily fished and brown trout from 0.5-3 kg can be taken on fly, spinner or live bait. This river is well stocked, easily waded and in favourable conditions an excellent evening rise occurs. Favoured locations include Wardells Bridge, east of Masterton, the cliffs area just south of Masterton, Te Whiti Bridge and Ponatahi Bridge. In the headwaters above Mt Bruce there is always the chance of a trophy fish. From Mt Bruce downstream to Masterton, the river is very unstable and subjected to shingle extraction. Below Tuhitarata, the river is deep, slow flowing and sluggish, but local anglers achieve results by slow trolling the river from a boat. A few large sea-run browns up to 6 kg enter the river during February and March but these are hard to catch. Perch up to 1 kg are present in the river as far up as Masterton, and will take any variety of trout lure.

In a fresh, the river rapidly becomes silt laden and takes time to clear. Try Caddis, Red Tipped Governor, Willow Grub, and Dark Hare and Copper nymphs, Dad's Favourite, Coch-y-bondhu and Twilight Beauty dry flies, or Hamill's Killer and small Yellow Rabbit lures. For the spin angler, Veltic, Meps and Cobra take fish. The lower reaches are generally fished with spinning gear while the upper reaches offer good fishing for the adventurous angler prepared to walk.

Location   Rises in the Tararua Ranges north-west of Masterton, flows in a southerly direction just east of Masterton and eventually empties into Lake Onoke at Palliser Bay.

Access
● *Upper reaches*   Flows parallel to, but east of, S.H.2 from Mt Bruce to Masterton. The stretch above this in the bush-covered Tararuas can only be reached by tramping across private farmland, and permission should be obtained.
● *Middle reaches*   From the Masterton–Gladstone road; from Papawai and Morrison's Bush south-east of Greytown; and from Martinborough.
● *Lower reaches*   From the Martinborough–Lake Ferry road.

Season   Open season on this river from 1 October to 30 September.

Waiohine River

This is an interesting river for the more energetic angler, especially in the upper reaches above Woodside where an occasional trophy fish can be anticipated. There are two bush-covered gorges, high bluffs and some deep holes before the river becomes more sedate, flowing over farmland before joining the Ruamahanga. The middle reaches from Woodside to S.H.2 are unstable, having been subjected to catchment activity. The lower reaches below S.H.2 offer good fishing down to the Ruamahanga confluence. The banks are willow lined, the river bed shingle and the water large. Boots and shorts are recommended for the upper reaches but the lower reaches can be comfortably waded. The water originates from stable bush-clad country, flows over a shingle bed and is usually clear. Brown trout up to 2 kg can sometimes be spotted and taken on fly or spinner. Live bait is not permitted.

Location   Drains the Tararuas west of Carterton, flows in an easterly direction south of the town to join the Ruamahanga east of Greytown.

Access
● *Upper reaches*   Take the road to Walls Whare and the Waiohine Gorge from S.H.2 south of Carterton. This leads to Joseph's Road, west of Matawara, and to the Tararua Forest Park.
● *Middle and lower reaches*   The river crosses S.H.2 just north of Greytown. Swamp Road, on the true left bank, and roads running west from Greytown provide easy access.

Season   Open 1 October — 30 September.

Mangatarere Stream

Fly fishing only on this small tributary of the Waiohine. Best fished early in the season from October to December before weed growth develops. It is a major spawning and nursery stream for the Ruamahanga system. There is 10 km of easily accessible water.

Location and access   From Carrington north of Carterton.

Waingawa River

A similar river to the Waiohine, but holds less water. Fish tend to be smaller and the river is not as well stocked as the Waiohine. The headwaters are very popular for tramper-anglers. Fish can be spotted and stalked with dry fly or nymph. Fish can be hooked on a weighted Hare and Copper nymph. Below Kaituna the river is unstable.

Location   Drains the Tararuas north-west of Masterton and flows in a south-easterly direction to join the Ruamahanga River 9 km south of that township.

Access
- *Upper Reaches*   Take Renall Street west from Masterton. This leads to Kaituna and the Tararua Forest Park.
- *Middle and lower reaches*   Crosses S.H.2 just south of Masterton. Norfolk Road follows up the true right bank before becoming the Mt Holdsworth road.

Season   Open 1 October — 30 September.

Waipoua River

This is a small tributary with easy access offering interesting water for the dry fly and nymph angler. But the catch rate is not high, and fish tend to be in the 0.5–1 kg range. There are some pleasant riffles and pools. Use small flies in the 14–16 range and fine tippets. Two small tributaries, the Mikimiki and the

Waingawa River, Wairarapa.

Kiriwhakapapa, also offer pleasant small stream fly fishing early in the season. All three streams flow across farmland, are willow lined and have shingle beds.

Location   Rises near Mount Bruce, flows in a south-easterly direction parallel to, but west of, S.H.2, and joins the Ruamahanga just east of Masterton.

Access   From Mikimiki and Paerau Roads which leave S.H.2 north of Masterton near Upper Opaki.

Season   1 October — 30 April. Fly fishing only is permitted upstream from Mikimiki Bridge.

Kopuaranga River

This spring-fed stream which meanders across swampy farmland is highly regarded as a dry fly and nymph stream. Browns in the 0.5–1.5 kg range can be anticipated, but fish stocks are not high. The lower and middle reaches are recommended as above Mauriceville the stream is choked by willows. The water is clear so a careful approach is essential. Mayfly, caddis and stone-fly imitations bring success.

Location   Rises just south of Eketahuna, flows in a southerly direction following the railway line to join the Ruamahanga at Opaki, 5 km north of Masterton.

Access   Turn right off S.H.2 just north of Opaki on the road to Kopuaranga and Mauriceville. There is easy access off this road and from side roads.

Season   1 October — 30 April. Fly fishing only is permitted in this stream.

Tauweru River

This river is not highly rated because it's willow infested, but the lower reaches hold good fish early in the season and are worth exploring.

Location and access   Flows in a southerly direction east of Masterton to join the Ruamahanga at Gladstone just upstream from the bridge over the Ruamahanga on the Gladstone–Carterton road.

Tauherenikau River

The upper reaches hold an occasional good fish. The middle and lower reaches are unstable and often dry in summer. However, the lower 2 km before it enters Lake Wairarapa hold fish, as does the shingle delta at the mouth. This is best fished at night with a black fly.

Location   Rises in the southern Tararuas and flows in a southerly direction to cross S.H.2 between Greytown and Featherston. Empties into Lake Wairarapa.

Access   S.H.2 and S.H.53 east of Featherston cross this river. Underhill and Bucks Roads, north of Featherston, give access to the upper reaches. Also, from Kaitoke on S.H.2 there is a tramping track to the upper reaches which can be reached in 1 hour.

Lake Wairarapa holds both brown trout and perch but is heavily silt laden and more suited to spinning. There are a few stream mouths along the western shore that can be fished at night but the area is not highly recommended.

Huangarua River

Shingle, willow-lined stream that dries during the summer but holds fish in the lower reaches early in the season.

Location   Flows in a northerly direction to join the Ruamahanga at Martinborough.

Access   From the Ponatahi and Hinakura roads.

Otakura Stream

This stream resembles a drain of brownish slow-moving water with grassy banks. On a calm, hot sunny day large brown trout can just be seen and stalked with a dry fly in the lower 1 km of water. Fish over 4 kg have been regularly taken by one skilful angler.

Location   Flows into Lake Wairarapa.

Access   From Featherston, follow Lake Ferry Road and turn off down Diversion Road. Permission must be obtained from the landowner at the end of the road.